ETERNAL SECURITY

CHARLES STANLEY

ETERNAL SECURITY

CAN YOU BE SURE?

OLIVER
NELSON

A Division of Thomas Nelson Publishers
Nashville

Published in Nashville, Tennessee, by Oliver-Nelson Books, a division of Thomas Nelson, Inc., Publishers, and distributed in Canada by Lawson Falle, Ltd., Cambridge, Ontario.

Scripture quotations are from the New American Standard Bible, © 1960, 1962, 1963, 1968, 1971, 1972, 1973, 1975, 1977 by The Lockman Foundation. Used by permission.

Scripture quotations noted NIV are taken from the HOLY BIBLE: NEW INTERNATIONAL VERSION. Copyright © 1973, 1978, 1984 by the International Bible Society. Used by permission of Zondervan Bible Publishers.

Scripture quotations noted KJV are from The King James Version of the Holy Bible.

Printed in the United States of America.

Library of Congress Cataloging-in-Publication Data

Stanley, Charles F.
    Eternal security / Charles Stanley.
      p. cm.
    Includes bibliographical references.
    ISBN 0-8407-9095-3
    1. Salvation. 2. Assurance (Theology) 3. Perseverance (Theology)
I. Title.
BT752.S73   1990
234—dc20
                                     90-40165
                                      CIP

4 5 6 — 95 94 93 92 91 90

Acknowledgment

I am grateful to my son, Andy, whose diligent research and keen insight made this book possible.

*Lovingly dedicated
to my father-in-law,
David A. Johnson,
who left this world
in August 1986,
eternally secure.*

Contents

Introduction

I have not always believed in eternal security. I was raised in the Pentecostal Holiness church, a denomination that did not believe in eternal security and frequently preached against it. As a child, I was not threatened by such preaching. I always loved church. I would arrive early to claim my second-row aisle seat—right in front of the pastor.

There were two reasons I chose to attend the Pentecostal Holiness church. First, my grandfather was a Pentecostal pastor. Second, it was my mother's preference. I can remember as a young boy getting up on Sunday morning, eating breakfast, and walking to church. Even when my mother was unable to go, I would be there.

June was typically revival month back in those days. In June of 1944 our evangelist for the week was a Mrs. Wilson. Women evangelists were not uncommon in the Pentecostal Holiness church. As was my habit, I was there Sunday morning, front and center, with every intention of attending each night that week. After the choir finished their song, Mrs. Wilson walked to the pulpit and preached a stirring salvation message. I don't remember anything in particular that she said; I just remember feeling a strong desire to respond. When the invitation began, I rose from my seat and went forward. Before I reached the altar, I began weeping. I knelt down and started asking Jesus to save me. Several members of my Sunday school class gathered around me and began praying for me as well.

When the altar call ended, the pastor of the church asked me to step up to the pulpit and share with the congregation what Christ had done for me. Still crying, I stood behind the pulpit and said, "I don't know all Jesus has done for me, but I know He saved me."

The pastor put his hand on my shoulder, looked at me square in the eye, and said, "Charles, grow up and be a good boy. And when you die, you will go to heaven."

Easier Said Than Done

It didn't take me long to realize that being good wasn't easy. To compound the problem, just about everything a twelve-year-old boy considered fun was a sin according to the Pentecostal Holiness church. I was continually confessing my sins, begging for forgiveness, and hoping I wouldn't die before I had time to repent!

During that time I began sensing God's call in my life. That meant one of two things in those days, becoming a preacher or a missionary. The awareness of God's call in my life only darkened the cloud of guilt under which I lived. *How could I ever help anybody else when I'm constantly wavering?* I would wonder. *What if I stood to preach and wasn't even saved?*

At age fourteen I joined the Baptist church. My decision was purely a social one. The Baptist church had a larger youth group than the Pentecostal church, and that meant more girls! That was when I discovered not everybody believed as I did. I first heard the phrase "eternal security" in that little Baptist church. Even as a teenager I was a diligent student of God's Word. Armed with my list of verses, I was prepared and even eager to present my side of the issue. No one made a dent in my theology. And I never expected anyone to, because I knew the Scripture was clearly on my side.

When I left home for college, I was still a staunch believer in the doctrine that one could lose his salvation.

2

Often in our dorm the conversation would turn to religion. Over and over I would pull out my arsenal of verses and present my case. Frequently, I found myself standing alone. But my view was strengthened by the carnal lifestyles of many with whom I debated, men who claimed to be saved and yet whose actions gave no indication of their having a relationship with Christ. Intellectually, I was more persuaded than ever. But deep inside a battle was raging.

Despite my strong defense and quiver of verses, I couldn't make it all fit. The events of that Sunday morning in 1944 were fixed in my memory. I remember for the first time feeling that I was at peace with God. I knew I had been born again. The possibility that I could lose all I had gained that Sunday morning seemed a little farfetched. And the idea that I could lose it and regain it repeatedly was difficult to comprehend.

Although I was troubled by my internal struggles, I never felt alienated from God. I had an inner peace even at my lowest times. Somehow I knew He still loved me and accepted me. My repeated requests for salvation were more a ritual than a heartfelt sense of need. I never felt lost. Yet the Scripture seemed to be so clear on that point. Consequently, I remained resolute in my defense.

Seminary Days

In the fall of 1954 I entered Southwestern Theological Seminary. Once again I found myself in heated discussions concerning the issue of eternal security. I continued my study of what I considered the pertinent passages of Scripture. For a long time I did not understand how anybody could think the Bible taught that the believer was eternally secure. But slowly that began to change.

Strangely enough, it was my intense study of the Scriptures that caused me to begin doubting my position. This was not a sudden change. It took time. Nobody convinced me. On the contrary, after a while nobody even wanted to talk to me about it; I had pretty much run the issue into the ground by that point. But as convincing as I was, I had no peace about the subject. So I continued to study.

Verse by verse I picked my way through the passages used to support each view. Through this process two things became apparent. First, I was guilty of ignoring the context of many verses I quoted to defend my view. As I began digging deeper into the events and discussions surrounding these passages, they took on a different meaning.

Second, I discovered through my study that the concept of salvation through faith alone cannot be reconciled with the belief that one can forfeit his or her salvation. If I must do or not do something to keep from losing my salvation, salvation would be by faith *and works.* I specifically remember the day this particular truth dawned on me. I found myself at a theological fork in the road. To maintain my position, I realized I would have to abandon my belief in salvation by faith alone.

It was as if a light came on. Suddenly I saw it. I wanted to shout. I felt like a man just freed from prison. I began to thank God that I had been wrong all those years. I thanked Him for the restlessness that had kept me searching and praying. Then I was struck with the most awesome thought of all. I had been eternally secure since that day as a twelve-year-old when I prayed, asking Jesus to save me.

That morning was a turning point in my life. It was far more than simply a shift in my theology. It introduced me to the true meaning of unconditional love. It was the beginning of my lifelong journey into the mystery of God's truly amazing grace. Terms such as *peace* and *joy* took on a whole new meaning. They became part of my experience, not just my vocabulary.

I realized how little I had really trusted God. You see, it is difficult to trust someone when you are never really sure where you stand with that person. *Security* came to mean a great deal more than a guarantee of where I would spend eternity. It was the perfect word to describe the sense of intimacy I felt with Christ. I was secure. Secure in His love and acceptance of me. Secure in His daily will for my life. Secure in every promise He had made. And of course, secure in where I would spend eternity.

I'm Not Alone

I continually meet people who believe as I once believed. If it were simply a theological difference, I would be content to agree to disagree. It is far more than that. I know the bondage to which that kind of thinking leads. I have lived with the guilt and the fear fostered by that view. Jesus said, "And you shall know the truth, and the truth shall make you free" (John 8:32). Freedom comes from knowing the truth. Bondage results from missing it.

The following pages are written in hopes that you will be set free to enjoy the relationship God has paid so dearly to provide. It is a relationship from which fear and worry are absent. I know from experience that until you settle once and for all the question of whether or not you are eternally secure, this quality of joy will elude you. Therefore, it is my prayer that God will use this book in your life and that in the very near future you will be able to face life with the confidence that comes through knowing you are eternally secure!

1

What Is at Stake?

Through the years I have enjoyed a unique privilege as the pastor of the First Baptist Church of Atlanta. Every time I deliver a message I know the truth is going out not only to my home congregation but to hundreds of other people as well. Through our "In Touch" television and radio ministry, I am able to reach out beyond the four walls of our sanctuary into living rooms, bedrooms, dens, hotel rooms, prisons, and many other places across America and into some foreign countries.

Along with this great privilege comes an awesome responsibility to ensure that every time someone turns to "In Touch," the truth is being offered. I learned a long time ago that people are not interested in my opinion. Neither are they interested in listening to *sermonettes,* short speeches on how good everything and everybody is. Least of all, people do not want a rehash of the latest news.

People are starving for God's truth to be made applicable to their situations. People want to know how to live, how to take the Bible and apply it to their daily lives. So every Monday morning I begin my week on my knees praying, "O Lord, what do You have for *me* this week?" And second, "Father, how do I make this clear to others?"

One of the most encouraging things about our television ministry has been its interdenominational appeal. Every week we receive letters from members of many denominations, Protestant and non-Protestant alike.

This kind of response says two things to me. First, people do not feel threatened by the fact that our ministry is that of a Baptist church. I am obviously not trying to make Baptists out of everyone. Second, our viewers trust that we have no hidden agenda. That is, we do not have a creed or specialized doctrinal stance that we are trying to sneak in under the guise of biblical preaching. People know that when they watch "In Touch," they are going to receive a practical lesson right out of the Scriptures.

However, as much as I enjoy the trust and acceptance of so many believers from such diverse denominational backgrounds, I never want to be guilty of soft-pedaling any particular biblical doctrine for the sake of maintaining people's approval. I have seen other ministries make that mistake. Their financial obligations grow to such magnitude that they literally cannot *afford* to lose any of their listening audience. This is one of the reasons we have chosen to grow slowly. Finances may determine the number of people we reach but never the message with which we reach them.

All of that is to say, I knew from the outset of this project that printing what I believe the Bible says about eternal security could possibly alienate some dear brothers and sisters in Christ. That is certainly not my intention. People who have listened to "In Touch" for any length of time know this is not something new to me. My testimony bears witness that I have held this view since my seminary days. Yet I reject the notion that eternal security is just a *Baptist doctrine.* As you read, I believe it will become apparent that this doctrine is first and foremost a biblical one. It is Baptist only in the sense that Baptists have included it in their doctrinal beliefs.

In spite of the negative feedback I anticipate receiving, I am going to forge ahead. Why? Because there is a great deal at stake here. The question of whether or not salvation is forever is not an isolated one. One's answer to this question affects every facet of one's theology. But this question goes beyond the realm of theology alone. It invades our Monday mornings. It creeps into our prayers. It shows up in our response to success and failure. It will hang over the deathbeds of our loved ones. Yes, there is a great deal at stake here.

If this issue were simply a theological hobbyhorse, I would leave it for a more capable theologian to ride. And certainly there are more complete works on the subject available. But this book is not intended as a theological discourse. This book is about love—love that found its most complete expression in Christ. This book is about grace—grace that knows no limits. This book is about God's insatiable desire to restore once and for all His broken relationship with His prize creation—you and me.

Assurance

Several things are at stake. First of all, our assurance. If our salvation hinges on anything but the finished work of Christ on the cross, we are in trouble. Or, at best, we run the risk of being in trouble. If you and I have any part in maintaining our salvation, it will be difficult to live with much assurance. Hope, yes; assurance, no.

Yet John wrote an entire epistle to assure a group of people, people he was not even around to observe, that they were in fact saved:

These things I have written to you who believe in the name of the Son of God, *in order that you may know* that you have eternal life.   —*1 John 5:13, emphasis mine*

Where there is no assurance of God's acceptance, there is no peace. Where there is no peace, there is no joy. Where there is no joy, there is a limitation on one's ability to love unconditionally. Why? Because a person with no assurance is by definition partially motivated by fear. Fear and love do not mingle well. One will always dilute the other.

Think About It

*If Christ
came to seek and to save
that which was lost,
and yet we can somehow
become unsaved—and therefore
undo what Christ came to do—
would it not be wise
for God to take us on to heaven
the moment we are saved
in order to insure we make it?
Isn't it unnecessarily risky
to force us to stay here?*

Furthermore, fear spills over into worry. Let's be realistic for a moment. If my salvation is not a settled issue, how can I be anxious for nothing (see Phil. 4:6)?

Forgiveness

Also at stake here is the extent of God's forgiveness. When Christ died, which of your sins did He die for? Which sins were you forgiven of when you trusted Him as Savior? If the sins you commit after becoming a Christian can annul your relationship with the Savior, clearly those sins were not covered at Calvary. Forgiven is forgiven. To differentiate between forgiven and unforgiven sins is to make a distinction foreign to Scripture. The timing of your sins is irrelevant since they were all in the future from the perspective of the Cross. To disregard eternal security is to take away from what happened at Calvary.

Faith Alone

Salvation by faith is at stake. Once good works are introduced into the salvation process, salvation is no longer by faith alone; it is by faith and works. To imply that salvation is maintained by good works (or not sinning) is to take the daily burden of our salvation upon ourselves. In that case, there will be room for boasting in heaven.

Saying that God's grace enables us to maintain good works will not solve this dilemma. For who is responsible for daily appropriating that grace? We are back where we began. If salvation is not forever, salvation cannot be through faith alone.

Love

If abandoning the faith or falling into sin short-circuits salvation, I have the ability to demonstrate unconditional love to a greater extent than God. If there is a condition—

even one—attached to God's willingness to maintain a relationship with His children, it is not unconditional. On the other hand, I know many people who have demonstrated pure unconditional love to family members who were incredibly undeserving.

One might argue, "But God's holiness demands certain things of those with whom He maintains a relationship. His nature will not allow Him to stay in a relationship with an individual who continually spurns His love."

That is beside the point. If His holiness demands something in return from those He loves, it is clear that His holiness makes God incapable of unconditional love! If holiness is a condition, His love is not unconditional. If His nature forces Him to disassociate from certain types of people, His nature stands in the way of His ability to love unconditionally.

Evangelism

Christians who are insecure about where they stand with God have a difficult time sharing the love of God with others. They often find it impossible to get beyond their own struggle with salvation. Not everyone who rejects the notion of "once saved, always saved" has this problem. But I have met many for whom this barrier is real.

Robert was a good example of this. He was consumed with the question of eternal security. Every time I spoke with Robert he somehow turned the conversation in that direction. I would see him coming and be tempted to run or to busy myself with something else. It was always the same thing. "Dr. Stanley, what about this verse in . . ."

I bring up Robert because he is a tragic illustration of something I see quite often: a person who becomes so absorbed with one issue that he gets out of balance. For some reason, eternal security seems to be one of those unbalancing issues. It is interesting as well as sad to see how often a person's evangelistic zeal suffers when this happens.

Focus

As long as I have an ongoing role in the salvation process, my natural tendency will be to focus on my behavior rather than on Christ. Yet we are commanded to make Christ our focus (see Phil. 4:8; Col. 3:2; Heb. 12:1–2). Certainly there is a place for self-examination in the Christian life.[1] But we are certainly not to be the *focus* of our lives. We are never completely free to fasten our gaze on Him until we are sure our relationship with Him is secure.

My observation has been that the more a person focuses on himself, the less he is able to keep his life in order. On the other hand, the more an individual focuses on Christ, the easier it becomes to allow Him to control every area of life.

People who are constantly examining their spiritual condition tend to fall into the trap of legalism. Legalism is almost always accompanied by two sidekicks: self-deception (calling sins by some other name so as to lessen the guilt) and pride. These go together to accomplish in a life the very opposite of what Christ intended.

Self-deception, accompanied by layer upon layer of denial, ultimately leads to greater and greater sin. Pride in these cases results in a critical spirit. Show me a believer who is caught up in trying to maintain God's acceptance through good works, and I will show you a fragile saint. My experience has been that these are the people who on the surface appear to be completely sold out to personal holiness and purity but who suddenly disappear. It is not unusual for these well meaning types to end up in a lifestyle completely opposite of what they once stood for. Such is the potential danger of a life lived without the assurance that salvation is forever.

In the Balance

These are just a few of the things affected by one's stance on the question of eternal security. This subject is not just something for theologians to bat about among themselves. This issue has a great deal to do with your life right now. Regardless of which view you are inclined to adopt, it will have a great impact on your perception of yourself, God, and others. For these reasons I feel compelled to write on this serious topic. For these same reasons I pray you will be compelled to read and reread until this issue is settled in your mind once and for all.

Notes

1. Some persons have used 2 Corinthians 13:5 to argue that a Christian must constantly "test" himself to see if he is really saved, which is not what Paul had in mind at all.

The context argues for the very opposite meaning. Paul is very confident of their salvation (see 2 Cor. 3:2–3). The emphatic placement of *you* in the Greek text indicates that he is encouraging them to recognize the salvation they clearly possess. They were checking themselves not for *information* but for *confirmation*.

See *The Expositors Bible Commentary* (Grand Rapids, Mich.: Zondervan, 1976), p. 403.

Do You Know?

1. *Why is the doctrine of eternal security more than a theological issue?*
2. *How would you answer the author's question, "If my salvation is not a settled issue, how can I be anxious for nothing?"*
3. *Why is the timing of your sins irrelevant?*
4. *What two "sidekicks" almost always accompany legalism?*

2

The Question at Hand

Problems must be properly defined before they can be solved. In this chapter we will survey the arguments raised by those who believe genuine salvation can be lost. Along the way we will take a brief tour of the history behind this belief. From there we will look at the divergence of opinion among the proponents of this view.

Historically Speaking . . .

Historically, this view has been associated with Arminian theology. Jacobus Arminius was a Dutch Reformed theologian who lived during the late sixteenth century. As a theologian, he found himself at odds with the Calvinistic teachings of his church. In particular, he took issue over the teachings on predestination, sovereignty, and eternal security.

Arminius believed that election was determined by man's response to God's universal offer of salvation. In other words, God looked through time and saw which of us would trust in His Son for salvation. He then elected the ones He knew would eventually choose Him. Since election hinged on man's response to God's offer, it followed that one could lose his elect status by later rejecting that offer. Consequently, there was no assurance of ultimate salvation.[1]

Arminians Today

Since the days of Arminius, many revered theologians and preachers, not the least of which was John Wesley, have espoused his views. Today the basic tenets of Arminianism are taught in the Nazarene church, the Wesleyan church, and the other denominations comprising the Christian Holiness Association.

Modern Arminianism falls within the realm of evangelicalism. That is, generally speaking, Arminians defend the deity of Christ, the virgin birth of Christ, the bodily resurrection of Christ, and the infallibility of Scripture.

Two Schools of Thought

As is the case with most doctrinal systems, there are differences among persons who would be considered Arminian in their theology. I have talked with literally hundreds of people about the question of eternal security. Some wanted to argue. Others sought answers. Through these discussions I have discovered that two schools of thought exist among those who believe salvation can be lost.

Abandoning the Faith

The first view falls within the framework of traditional Arminian theology. Simply stated, *a genuine born-again believer can lose his or her salvation by turning away from the Christian faith (i.e., by no longer believing or trusting in Christ).* Such a person would be considered an "apostate." *Apostasy* is defined as "a deliberate repudiation and abandonment of the faith that one has professed."[2] Individuals holding this view often interpret scriptural references to "falling away" as apostasy.[3]

Hebrews 6:4–6

The classic passage used to defend this view is found in the sixth chapter of Hebrews. Over the course of my ministry, people have more frequently asked me for help in interpreting this passage than any other passage in the Bible. And understandably so! Here is what it says:

> For in the case of those who have once been enlightened and have tasted of the heavenly gift and have been made partakers of the Holy Spirit, and have tasted the good word of God and the powers of the age to come, and then have *fallen away,* it is impossible to renew them again to repentance, since they again crucify to themselves the Son of God, and put Him to open shame. —*Hebrews 6:4–6, emphasis mine*

The issue for proponents of this view is *faith,* not necessarily *faithfulness.* There is room in their theology for temporary moral and ethical failure by the believer. The fact that a believer commits a sin is not necessarily a sign that he has lost his salvation. However, the man or woman who deliberately turns away from the church, Christ, and all that He stands for has surely stepped out of the kingdom of light back into the kingdom of darkness. After all, they argue, if we are free to choose Christ, are we not free to choose against Him?

The parable of the sower is used to illustrate this point (see Luke 8:4–15). The sower sows on different soils representing persons and their response to the truth. The soil beside the road is compared to the unbeliever. The rocky soil, however, is compared to the man who "[believes] for a while, and in time of temptation [falls] away" (v.13).

We have all met someone like that man depicted in the parable, someone who said, "Oh, I used to believe all that but not anymore." The person at one time genuinely believed. But something happened that caused him to turn his back on Christ; he no longer believes. According to

Think About It

*If our salvation is not secure,
how could Jesus say
about those to whom He gives
eternal life, "and they shall
never perish" (John 10:28)?
If even one man or woman
receives eternal life and
then forfeits it through sin
or apostasy, will they not perish?
And by doing so,
do they not make Jesus' words
a lie?*

those who do not believe in eternal security, the phrase "fall away" in this passage refers to the loss of salvation.[4]

The potential for losing salvation lies not only with those who have a rebellious heart toward God but with those who are innocently led astray by false doctrines as well. Paul expresses his amazement and concern over the Galatians "deserting" the truth and turning to "a different gospel" (Gal. 1:6). About this same group he later says,

> You have been severed from Christ, you who are seeking to be justified by law; you have fallen from grace. . . . You were running well; who hindered you from obeying the truth?
> —*Galatians 5:4, 7*

Notice Paul's strong language to describe the Galatians' present status: They are "severed from Christ" and "fallen from grace."

A similar situation surfaces in Paul's first letter to Timothy. Here Paul predicts that in the last days some believers will be tricked into following false doctrines:

> But the Spirit explicitly says that in later times some will *fall away* from the faith, paying attention to deceitful spirits and doctrines of demons, by means of the hypocrisy of liars seared in their own conscience as with a branding iron.
> —*1 Timothy 4:1–2, emphasis mine*

Once again the phrase "fall away" appears. Here the context clearly implies a turning away from the faith, a rejection of what was once fully embraced.

In these last two examples, the believers in question did not fall into "sin" in the moral or ethical sense. They were simply deceived into believing something that was a distortion of the truth. Yet these passages seem to indicate that the consequence of their naivete was eternal damnation.

19

Every Day Falling Away

Most of the folks I encounter who do not believe in eternal security are unclear about exactly how and when one loses salvation. By that I mean, they are not sure what it takes to lose it—they are just sure you can! As one fellow put it, "I know God is merciful, but He is not a fool." In other words, there must come a point when God says, "Enough is enough!" For most, if not all, proponents of this view, that point is very illusive and undefined.

Whereas the first group would reserve the loss of salvation for those who have clearly turned their backs on the Christian faith as a whole, the focus of this second group is the life-style or behavior of believers. According to this view, *a believer's security is based on his willingness to continually strive toward spiritual excellence.*[5] Didn't Paul exhort believers to "work out" their own salvation with "fear and trembling" (Phil. 2:12)? Why the inclusion of "fear and trembling"? Because he apparently believed the possibility of losing one's salvation was a real threat.

It Does Not Make Sense

Many people have drawn their conclusions concerning eternal security not from a scriptural standpoint but from a practical one. Let's go back to the young man who made the comment about God's being "merciful" but not a "fool." What motivates a statement like that? In his case he had given this thing concentrated thought. His line of reasoning went something like this:

1. God is a holy God and demands holiness from His children.
2. God is a merciful and forgiving God.
3. At some point in the life of a disobedient Christian, God's mercy runs out, and His holiness takes over.
4. At that point God deals with His child totally from the

standpoint of His demand for holiness and obedience.

5. This may result in placing a person back outside the circle of acceptance.

6. After all, God cannot accept what is contrary to His holy nature.

The idea of eternal security just did not make any sense to this young man. Why would God keep putting up with people who for all practical purposes could care less about Him or His Son? If individuals no longer believe, it is as if they have broken their salvation contract; they have not upheld their end of the deal. Is God under obligation to maintain a saving relationship with people who have that kind of attitude?

It Does Not Seem Fair

Another argument I have heard through the years focuses on the question of justice. Is it fair to allow "Christians" who went the way of the world to share in the same eternal blessing as those who followed Christ throughout their lives? Can a truly just God allow the faithful and the unfaithful to be equally rewarded? Besides, doesn't the Bible say that if we deny Him before men, He will deny us before the heavenly Father (see Matt. 10:33)? If a person makes it to heaven regardless of the type of life he or she leads, why strive to live in a godly manner?

The Fear Factor

Dovetailing into the question of justice is that of license. Many people are afraid of this doctrine. They see it as a potential excuse to live free from all restraint. A man said to me recently, "I don't believe we should preach about eternal security." When I asked him why, he said, "I don't think people can handle that kind of freedom." He meant that if Christians think they can do anything they want and still go to heaven, they will do just that! Every once in a while I run across people with that attitude. They have no intention of straightening up their lives. They see no need to. According to the doctrine of eternal security, they can have their cake and eat it, too. So why change? People with that attitude scare many away from the doctrine of eternal security. It just leaves things too open-ended.

"Saved, Yes. Heaven, Maybe."

My father-in-law was a wonderful man. He did not come to know the Lord until late in his life, but he made up for lost time. Visits and phone calls were packed full of questions about the Bible. He and his wife attended church three or four times a week. Right up until the day he died, he was growing spiritually by leaps and bounds. In spite of all that, however, he never had any assurance about his salvation.

I would ask him, "Mr. Johnson, are you sure you have trusted Christ as your Savior?"

"Oh, yes," he would reply. "He is living in my heart today."

I would continue, "So then you are sure if you were to die, you would go to heaven?"

"Now, I don't know about that," he would say.

Round and round we would go. But I could never convince him. His problem was not any particular passage of Scripture. He struggled with the question of how God could forgive him for the sins he committed before coming to faith. The idea of God's being that loving and forgiving was too much for him to comprehend. He was sure he was a Christian, but heaven was a different thing altogether.

I often meet people like my father-in-law. People who believe Christ died for their sins. Men and women who love God with all their hearts. But somehow they cannot accept with any certainty that God has forgiven them. One day they are sure of their salvation; the next day they are not. Back and forth they go, hoping they will make it but having no assurance.

Looking Ahead

What about you? What is the issue on your mind? Is it a passage of Scripture? Is it a personal experience that you just can't seem to erase from your memory? Have you been turned off by the way people use the concept of eternal security to excuse their sin? Were you raised to believe that the idea of "once saved, always saved" was something the Baptists or some other group just invented?

In the following pages we will look at these objections in detail. This is a heavy topic that calls for heavy answers. I will do my best to be both clear and thorough. If you find yourself getting lost in the details of certain chapters, bear with me. My goal is to anticipate both the questions and the objections that accompany this topic. If this work can answer even one of your questions and thereby move you one step closer to accepting the permanency of your salvation, it will have been worth the effort for both of us.

Notes

1. "Arminianism," in *Oxford Dictionary of the Christian Church,* 2d ed.; also "Arminianism," in *Evangelical Dictionary of Theology* (Grand Rapids, Mich.: Baker, 1984).
2. "Apostasy," in *Evangelical Dictionary of Theology.*
3. Dale Moody, *The Word of Truth,* (Grand Rapids, Mich.: Eerdmans, 1981), pp. 348–49.
4. Moody, *Word of Truth,* pp. 348–49.
5. Moody, *Word of Truth,* p. 351.

Do You Know?

1. *Who was the the sixteenth century Dutch Reformed theologian who took issue with the Calvinist doctrines of predestination, sovereignty, and eternal security? How did he believe salvation was determined?*
2. *What present-day churches teach the basic tenets of Arminianism?*
3. *What are the two schools of thought among those who believe salvation can be lost?*
4. *Why do some Christians feel that the doctrine of eternal security is too open-ended?*

3

Saved and Secure

Not too long ago a teenager in our church brought two of her friends to meet me. I felt impressed to ask them about their salvation. "Have you both been saved?" I asked. They both nodded that they had. I took it a step further. "Tim," I said, "tell me about it." He related his experience of going forward in a service, praying with an elder, and being presented to the congregation. "Darla," I said, speaking to the other guest, "why should God let you into heaven?" She looked down. "Well, I don't know. I don't go to church very much anymore. But I sure like your church," she said.

I knew I had made them both a little uncomfortable. So I talked to them about my own struggle with that question. I showed them a couple of verses that made it clear how we can know we are saved. Then I asked them again, "So, why do you think God should let you into heaven?" Tim spoke up, "Because I believe in God and try to do my best."

I had to laugh. *Lord,* I thought to myself, *how many people sit out here week after week who would claim in a heartbeat that they are saved, but haven't the foggiest idea how they got that way?*

"Tim," I said, "sometimes I don't explain this very well. Let me try again." We went through another round of verses, complete with my best illustrations.

After twenty minutes Tim shot straight up in his chair and said, "It's because His death paid for my sins!" It was

25

as if someone had turned on a switch in his mind. Actually someone had! Both Tim and Darla trusted Christ as their Savior that evening. As we were getting up to go, Darla said, "I never heard it explained like that. I'm so glad I came."

First Things First

Before we can proceed any further with our discussion, we need to grasp one important point. What do we mean by *salvation?* The question we are addressing in this book is whether or not salvation can be lost. We would do well to understand exactly what it is we are arguing cannot be lost!

If a man's or woman's understanding on this question is as foggy as Tim's or Darla's, he or she has good reason to doubt the doctrine of eternal security. *Where there is uncertainty concerning how salvation is attained, there will be confusion over whether it can be maintained.*

My experience has been that those who have problems with the doctrine of eternal security have a distorted understanding of what took place at the Cross. That may sound as if I am being critical. But in reality I am more puzzled than anything else. When I think of Calvary, and the price that was paid to provide me with salvation, the thought of my having the power to undo all of that seems preposterous.

Salvation

Sin brought about the need for man's salvation. Sin is like a genetic disease that, once introduced into the human race, affected everyone thereafter:

> Therefore, just as through one man sin entered into the world, and death through sin, and so death spread to *all men,* because all sinned. —*Romans 5:12, emphasis mine*

26

The "one man" here is Adam. His sin poisoned the human race. Every man, woman, and child since Adam was born a sinner:

> For as through the one man's disobedience the many were made sinners. —*Romans 5:19*

Rotten to the Core

Sin goes deeper than merely an association with some distant relative. Sin has contaminated our very nature. Man is born with an inclination toward evil, a bias away from good. If you don't believe me, ask any preschool worker or kindergarten teacher. Children never need a lesson in being bad. It comes naturally. Granted, some are worse than others. But each child in his or her own way eventually demonstrates a defiant self-centeredness willing to challenge any and all authority.

The combination of our inherent sinfulness and our ensuing acts of sin puts us in bad standing with God. The Bible goes so far as to say we are condemned:

> And the gift is not like that which came through the one who sinned; for on the one hand the judgment arose from one transgression resulting in *condemnation.* —*Romans 5:16, emphasis mine*

The term *condemn* is a legal term meaning "to declare guilty." We are each guilty of *sin*—resulting from our relation with Adam—and *sins*—resulting from our personal disobedience.

The Result

Just as sin caused Adam and Eve to be separated from God in the beginning, so sin results in man's separation from God now and potentially for eternity. Paul writes,

Think About It

*Why should God let you
into heaven? If your answer
includes words such as* try,
my best, church, believe in God,
Sunday school, teach, *or* give,
*chances are that you still
haven't come to grips with
the simple truth that salvation
is by faith* alone.

*Let me ask the question
another way. What are you
trusting in to get you
into heaven? Is it Christ*
plus *something? Or can you say
with confidence that
your hope and your trust
are in Christ
and Christ alone?*

For the wages of sin is death.　　　　　　*—Romans 6:23*

And again,

For all have sinned and fall short of the glory of God.
　　　　　　　　　　　　　　　　—Romans 3:23

These familiar passages say a great deal about the consequences of sin. When the Bible speaks of death, it does not refer to annihilation. Nowhere does the Scripture teach the annihilation of the soul. *Everyone* will live forever, somewhere. Death means separation, specifically, separation from God.

The second verse explains *why* sinners must die, or be separated from God. Our sin makes us ineligible for perfection. God is holy and pure in nature. He is the essence of love and goodness. Those who are to have fellowship with Him must be holy and pure as well. They must be guiltless, guilty of no sin whatsoever. His nature demands it. His nature, by definition, determines the standard for those who desire a relationship with Him. To put it another way, certain things must be true of people to make them acceptable to God.

This is not some arbitrary set of rules God established to make it difficult for us. If that were so, Christ died in vain. God should have just changed the rules. But God's high standard flows from His unalterable nature. And man has fallen short of that standard.

God's holiness can be compared to fire. Certain things must be true of any material that is to survive being exposed to fire. The nature of fire determines what will and will not endure the heat. God's holiness can be compared to water. Certain things must be true of any animal that is to live underwater. The nature of water demands that these things be true. Any animal that is not suited to survive underwater will drown if held under the water.

Certain things must be true of the man or the woman

who intends to establish a relationship with holy God. There are changes to be made, changes that we are hopelessly incapable of making ourselves. Our sin has caused us to fall short of God's standard. Thus in our natural state, we are destined for a godless eternity.

Guilt Removal

The primary change that must be made centers on the problem of guilt. Salvation, at its core, is *the removal of guilt,* both personal and imputed.

Herein lies the problem. If God is perfect, He is perfectly just. How can a perfectly just God make a guilty person not guilty? As Dr. Ryrie says in *Basic Theology,*

> There are only three options open to God as sinners stand in His courtroom. He must condemn them, compromise His own righteousness to receive them just the way they are, or He can change them into righteous people. If He can exercise the third option, then He can announce them righteous, which is justification.[1]

Dr. Ryrie brings to our discussion a very important term, *justification.* To justify people is to declare them not guilty. In the book of Romans, Paul makes it clear that Christians have been justified (see 5:1). To him, there is no conflict between God's justice and His willingness to justify sinners. He says,

> For the demonstration . . . of His righteousness at the present time, that He might be *just* and the *justifier* of the one who has faith in Jesus.   —*Romans 3:26, emphasis mine*

God does not wear rose-colored glasses. He is not in the habit of pretending something is true when in fact it isn't. So how can He declare guilty men and women "not guilty"?

Paul sums up the answer to that question in his second letter to the Corinthians:

> He made Him [Jesus] who knew no sin to be sin on our behalf, that we might become the righteousness of God in Him.
> —*2 Corinthians 5:21*

God made a swap. Actually, the correct term is *imputation.* He imputed our sin to Christ and His righteousness to us. To impute something to people is to credit them with it. Christ credited us with His righteousness, including all its rights and privileges.

But there was still the problem of our sin. God could not remain just and ignore sin. There was a penalty to be paid. So Christ was credited with our sin. Consequently, He suffered death in our place and in doing so paid the penalty we had incurred.

"My God, My God"

You may be wondering, "If our sin demanded a death— but this death involved eternal separation from God— how could Christ pay the penalty for our sin and still sit at the Father's right hand? If He took our place, would He not have to be separated from God?"

The answer to that question is yes. For Christ to truly pay for our sins, He would have to suffer the punishment originally intended for us. And He did. Concerning the death of Christ, Mark says,

> And when the sixth hour had come, darkness fell over the whole land until the ninth hour. And at the ninth hour Jesus cried out with a loud voice, "Eloi, Eloi, lama sabachthani?" which is translated, "My God, My God, why hast Thou forsaken Me?"
> —*Mark 15:33–34*

As Christ hung on the cross, God abandoned Him. The separation was so real that Christ even addressed God differently. Until that time He had referred to God as His Father. Suddenly, however, the fellowship was broken, and Jesus shouted not "My Father" but "My God!" The intimacy was gone. Christ was alone.

The penalty of your sin was death, physically and spiritually. Sin demanded separation from life and God. And so Christ willingly paid that penalty in your place.

The awesomeness of God's plan cannot be fully appreciated until we understand how and why Christ was able to reestablish fellowship with His estranged heavenly Father. The writer of Hebrews explains,

> But when Christ appeared as a high priest of the good things to come, He entered through the greater and more perfect tabernacle, not made with hands, that is to say, not of this creation; and not through the blood of goats and calves but through His own blood, He entered the holy place once for all, having obtained eternal redemption.
> —*Hebrews 9:11–12*

After paying the penalty for our sin, Christ marched right back into the presence of God. How? What enabled fellowship to be restored? Christ's own righteousness. Sin is the barrier between man and God. Christ had no sin. Therefore, there was nothing to keep Christ from reuniting with the Father after a brief period of separation. Christ's sinlessness made Him the only acceptable sacrifice for sin.

Signing Up

Faith is the means by which the saving work of Christ is applied to the individual. Specifically, salvation comes to the individual when that person places trust in Christ's death on the cross as the complete payment for sin.

The biblical support for this idea comes from a grammatical construction that occurs repeatedly when faith is mentioned in connection with forgiveness and salvation. This construct consists of the Greek word that means "believe" followed by a little word translated "in" or "on," depending on the context of the passage. The combination of the term for "believe" and this little preposition is unique to the New Testament. In other words, the writers of the New Testament were forced to coin a new phrase to accurately communicate their unique message:[2]

> For this is the will of My Father, that everyone who beholds the Son and *believes in* Him, may have eternal life; and I Myself will raise him up on the last day.   —*John 6:40, emphasis mine*

> But as many as received Him, to them He gave the right to become children of God, even to those who *believe in* His name.
> —*John 1:12, emphasis mine*

> Now when He was in Jerusalem at the Passover during the feast, many *believed in* His name, beholding His signs which He was doing.   —*John 2:23, emphasis mine*

The gospel writers understood that Jesus was calling men to do more than simply believe in His existence. They knew from their own experience that Christ was calling on sinners to put their trust in Him: in His life, in His words, and ultimately in His death as payment for their sin.

Gaining "eternal life" and becoming "children of God" are the apostle John's terms for salvation. Paul prefers the term mentioned earlier—*justification:*

> Therefore having been *justified* by faith, we have peace with God through our Lord Jesus Christ.—*Romans 5:1, emphasis mine*

> But to the one who does not work, but *believes in* Him who *justifies* the ungodly, his faith is reckoned as righteousness.
> —*Romans 4:5, emphasis mine*

A Simple Plan for Sinful Man

God's plan is so simple:
- We are guilty.
- Our guilt earned us death.

- Christ died in our place.
- We admit we are guilty.
- We trust that Christ was punished in our place.
- We are declared "not guilty."

That's it! And yet *that* is what some argue we can lose. But how? How can I lose Christ's payment for my sin? Can God declare me "guilty" after He has already declared me "not guilty"?

But, Wait!

"But, wait," the skeptic counters, "what about the sins you commit after He declares you 'not guilty'?"

Good question. But think about it. Which of your sins did Christ take to the cross two thousand years ago? Which of your sins was He punished for? If He died for only part of your sins—for instance, the ones you had committed up to the point of salvation—how can you ever get forgiveness for the sins you commit after that? Would Christ not have to come and die again? And for that matter, again and again and again?

If all your sins were not dealt with on the cross two thousand years ago, there is no hope for you! God declared you "not guilty" the first time based on the provision of His Son. *On what basis could He declare you "not guilty" the second time?*

The next time Christ shows up on the earth His agenda will not include dying for the sins He missed the first time around (see Heb. 9:28). The Scripture is clear. Christ, unlike sheep and goats, needed to be offered up only once. And God accepted that as the once and for all sacrifice for all men's sin:

> [Christ entered] into heaven itself, now to appear in the presence of God *for us;* nor was it that He should offer Himself *often,* as the high priest enters the holy place year by year with blood not his own. Otherwise, He would have needed to suffer *often* since the foundation of the world; but now *once* at the consummation of

34

the ages He has been manifested to *put away sin* by the sacrifice of Himself. . . . So Christ also, having been offered *once* to bear the sins of many, shall appear a second time for salvation[3] without reference to sin.
 —*Hebrews 9:24–28, emphasis mine; see also 9:12*

From the historical vantage point of the Cross, all your sins were yet to be committed. If Christ died for one of them, He died for all of them. What was the difference? He need not come again to pay for sin. On that day He took upon Himself all the sin of mankind—past, present, and future.

How can anyone possibly undo all of that? If Christ took upon Himself every single one of your sins, what is going to cause God to reverse His verdict of not guilty?

Hallelujah, not a thing!

Notes

1. Charles C. Ryrie, *Basic Theology* (Wheaton, Ill.: Victor Books, 1987), pp. 298–99.
2. Gerald F. Hawthorne, "The Concept of Faith in the Fourth Gospel," *Bibliotheca Sacra,* April 1959.
3. "Salvation" here is not a reference to eternal salvation in the sense of saving a man from hell. The writer uses the term here to refer to the salvation of Christians from the catastrophic events that will take place on earth just prior to the Second Coming (see Heb. 1:14; 7:25).

Do You Know?

1. *How does sin contaminate human nature?*
2. *Why is it necessary for the sinner to die?*
3. *What does the term* imputation *mean?*
4. *Why was it necessary for Jesus to suffer separation from God?*
5. *What is it about Christ's nature that made Him the only acceptable sacrifice for sin?*
6. *What terms did the apostle John use for salvation? What term did the apostle Paul prefer?*
7. *If you are forgiven for all your sins you committed before you accepted salvation, what about the sins you commit later?*

4

Adoption

Justification has somewhat of a negative ring to it. When a judge pronounces a man "not guilty," that certainly does not necessitate a change in the nature of the judge's relationship with the defendant. In most cases the judge is hostile or, at best, apathetic about the whole ordeal. Ideally, there is nothing personal gained or lost from the judge's perspective.

The concepts of acquittal and forgiveness are certainly similar, but there are some important differences as well. To be acquitted of a crime is to be released from obligation concerning any debts or liabilities. Forgiveness includes that idea, but goes even further. To forgive someone is to accept the individual back into the realm of fellowship. Forgiveness implies the restoration of a relationship.

When men and women place their trust in Christ as their Savior, they are not simply acquitted of their sin; they are forgiven. One writer described the distinction this way:

> It is one thing for us to be pardoned, for the penalty incurred by our wrongdoing to have been paid. That, however, may simply mean we will not be punished in the future. It does not necessarily guarantee goodwill. If a criminal's debt to society has been paid, society will not thereafter look favorably or charitably upon him. There will instead be suspicion, distrust, even animosity. With the Father, however, there are the love and goodwill that we so desperately need and desire. He is ours, and we are His, and

He . . . extends to us all the benefits His measureless love can bestow.[1]

Children of God

The New Testament writers understood this distinction as well. As significant as the judicial side of our salvation is, they knew that to overlook the relational element would be to paint an unbalanced picture. Under the influence of the Holy Spirit, they each chose something from either their culture or their nature that would lend itself as an accurate illustration of this unique relationship between holy God and man.

The Holy Spirit directed the apostle Paul to use the term *adoption* to describe the process by which God establishes a relationship with a man or woman who trusts Christ as the Savior:

> For you have not received a spirit of slavery leading to fear again, but you have received a spirit of *adoption* as sons by which we cry out, "Abba! Father!" The Spirit Himself bears witness with our spirit that we are children of God.[2]
> *—Roman 8:15–16, emphasis mine*

Notice how Paul capitalizes on the relational value of adoption. We are encouraged to think of our heavenly Father in the most intimate way, as a Daddy. This relationship is contrasted to one of fear, which commonly existed between a slave and his master. God is not simply putting up with us as a master would with slaves. God desires an intimate relationship with us. And He has taken it upon Himself to remove every possible barrier.

Paul echoes the same idea in his letter to the Galatians:

> But when the fulness of the time came, God sent forth His Son, born of a woman, born under the Law, in order that He might redeem those who were under the Law, that we might receive the *adoption* as sons. *—Galatians 4:4–5, emphasis mine*

Here Paul makes the connection between adoption and justification. The interesting thing is that the grammar of these verses indicates that our justification was merely a means to an end. God's ultimate goal in salvation was the relationship made available through our adoption. Being declared "not guilty" was simply a necessary step in that direction.

Court Adjourned!

God does not intend for us to consider Him a stern Judge peering over the bench at the accused. Yet many believers have this very perception of Him. For some reason they never get out of the courtroom and into the family room. God is always a Judge, never a Father.

This view is so unfortunate. But even worse, it is a precursor to doubting the doctrine of eternal security. I've talked with Christians who live with the fear that the gavel may strike again—this time with a guilty verdict. The good news is that after the Judge pronounced you and me "not guilty," He walked from behind the bench and welcomed us into His family. The days of the courtroom are over. That is apparent from John's gospel:

> Truly, truly, I say to you, he who hears My word, and believes Him who sent Me, has eternal life, and *does not come into judgment,* but has passed out of death into life.
> —*John 5:24, emphasis mine*

As a believer, you will never be judged for your sins. That is a settled issue. It is so settled in the mind of God that at the moment of your salvation, knowing full and well all the sins you were yet to commit, God adopted you into His family.

Let me say again, adopting us into His family was not simply a courtesy God was extending to us poor wretched sinners. It was His goal from the very beginning. And not

Think About It

*If salvation wasn't permanent,
why introduce the concept
of adoption? Wouldn't it
have been better just to describe
salvation in terms
of a conditional legal contract
between man and God?*

just from *our* very beginning, but from the beginning of time, as these verses make plain:

> Blessed be the God and Father of our Lord Jesus Christ, who has blessed us with every spiritual blessing in the heavenly places in Christ, just as He *chose us in Him before the foundation of the world,* that we should be holy and blameless before Him. In love He *predestined us to adoption as sons* through Jesus Christ to Himself, according to the kind intention of His will.
> —*Ephesians 1:3–5, emphasis mine*

God chose to adopt you as His child before the foundation of the world. Why? For one reason and one reason only: He wanted to. That is what Paul means by the phrase, "according to the kind intention of His will." No one forced Him. God wanted you as His child. God did not send Christ to die because He felt sorry for you. He sacrificed His only begotten Son so that He could make you His adopted child.

I have heard of many unwanted pregnancies; I have never heard of an unwanted adoption. Couples adopt children because they *want* children. God adopted you for the same reason. He knew your shortcomings. He knew your inconsistencies. He knew all about you. But He wanted you just the same.

Back to the Courtroom

Paul's reliance on the concept of adoption is a strong argument for eternal security. To lose one's salvation, one would have to be unadopted! Within that system there must also be provision for readoption. The very idea sounds ludicrous. If the logistics of such a belief system are not enough to make you wonder, consider the relational problems such a system creates. Could you ever really put your total trust in a heavenly Father who may unadopt you?

Let me put it another way. Can we pledge unconditional

loyalty to a God who promises only conditional loyalty in return? Isn't it unrealistic to think that we could ever grow comfortable thinking of God as our Dad when we know that if we drift away or fall into sin, the relationship will be severed?

Persons holding to a view that allows for one to be unadopted must confront another major theological hurdle. *Why would God choose before the foundation of the world to adopt someone He knew He would eventually have to unadopt?* To believe we can be unadopted is to believe that man is able to thwart the predestined will of God! Or it is to believe that something in the nature of God forces Him to unadopt certain types of children.

I have met and worked with teenagers and young adults who, because of unfortunate circumstances, were passed around from foster home to foster home. The emotional and mental damage is devastating. Self-esteem is almost nonexistent. Their environment has bred into them a deep sense of insecurity. The only thing I have seen really work for kids with this background is overpowering love, the kind that takes them from wherever they are and sticks with them through all the necessary stages of recovery.

Excuse me if I sound overdramatic, but people who believe they can lose their positions as children of God are set up for a serious case of spiritual insecurity. How deep can my relationship with God really go when He cannot or will not pledge to me His unconditional love and acceptance?

Hope for the Best

If the former is true, we better cross our fingers and *hope* Christ ultimately defeats the Antichrist in the end. If mortal man can thwart God's prophetic will for his own life, think of what a supernaturally empowered world leader could do on a universal scale! What is the difference? Both Ephesians 1 and the book of Revelation describe God's ultimate intentions. How can we have absolute faith in one when we allow for exceptions in the other?

On the other hand, if something in the nature of God forces His hand, so to speak, we are actually saved by faith and works! How so? If there are certain sins that force God to unadopt His children, our salvation is contingent on our *faith* and our *willingness* not to commit those particular sins (whatever they may be). Furthermore, it means Christ did not take every sin with Him to the cross.

As you can see, the very foundations of Christianity begin to crumble once we begin tampering with the eternal security of the believer. There is no scriptural support for the notion that the adoption process can be reversed. On the contrary, in the next chapter we will see an illustration of just how permanent it really is.

Notes

1. Millard J. Erickson, *Christian Theology* (Grand Rapids, Mich.: Baker, 1985), p. 965.
2. Some understand the conditional nature of verse 17 to imply that we are only children *if* we "suffer with Him." The "if" of verse 17 is translated from the Greek word *eiper* which denotes more the idea of "since" than "if" (see Rom. 8:9). For other examples of this use, refer to Bauer, Gingrich, and Danker's work, *A Greek-English Lexicon of the New Testament and Other Early Christian Literature* (Chicago: University of Chicago Press, 1958), p. 220.

Do You Know?

1. *What is the difference between* acquittal *and* forgiveness?
2. *What did the apostle Paul mean by the term* adoption?
3. *What one reason does the author give for God's choosing to adopt you as His child?*
4. *How does the author come to the conclusion that if certain sins could force God to "unadopt his children," it would mean that Christ did not take every sin with Him to the cross?*
5. *Is there any scriptural support for the notion that the adoption process can be reversed?*

5

Is Adoption Forever?

If our salvation can be lost, our adoption into the family of God is not permanent. We can be unadopted, so to speak. Such a process, however, is never described or even alluded to in the New Testament. Never once are believers threatened with losing membership in the family of God. Jesus taught just the opposite. As far as He was and is concerned, adoption is forever!

A Differing Opinion

The religious leaders of Jesus' day did not share this conviction. They did not hold to the doctrine of eternal security. They believed righteousness was gained and maintained through keeping the Mosaic law. According to their theology, if a man abandoned the law, God abandoned him. That belief deeply affected their attitude and behavior toward persons who were not keeping the law in the manner the leaders thought they should. As religious leaders and shepherds of the people, they took it upon themselves to visibly model God's disdain for those who did not keep the law. Consequently, they would have nothing to do with certain classes of people.

For that reason it was not uncommon to hear a Pharisee praying the way Jesus described:

> And He also told this parable to certain ones who trusted in themselves that they were righteous, and viewed others with

contempt: "Two men went up into the temple to pray, one a
Pharisee and the other a tax-gatherer. The Pharisee stood and
was praying thus to himself, 'God, I thank Thee that I am not like
other people: swindlers, unjust, adulterers, or even like this tax-
gatherer. I fast twice a week; I pay tithes of all that I get.' "[1]

—Luke 18:9–12

The Pharisee looked down on those who were not as
"committed" or "disciplined" as he was. In his way of
thinking, he was simply mirroring God's attitude. That distorted view of God's attitude compelled Christ on several
occasions to focus His teaching on the subject.

Despite His clear teaching, some people are still confused. This confusion has driven some away from believing in eternal security. Like the Pharisees of old, some
Christians believe their eternal security rests not on the
finished work of Christ at Calvary but on the consistency
of their good works. To put it another way, they have been
adopted into the family of God by grace; but whether or
not they remain in the family hinges on their willingness
to act like family members. They live with the threat of
being unadopted.

A Wonderful Accusation

On one occasion Jesus was being swamped by tax gath-
erers and sinners. And His interaction with them really got
under the skin of the religious leaders. They could not
figure out how a Teacher who claimed to be from God
could fellowship with those whom they believed God dis-
dained. They began to complain to one another, "This
man receives sinners and eats with them" (Luke 15:2).
Sharing a meal in that culture was a sign of acceptance
and genuine fellowship.

Jesus knew their thoughts and took the opportunity to
draw their attention to the error of their thinking through
a series of parables. In each parable something precious

was lost. And in each parable the owner put aside everything else and focused attention on finding it.

In the first parable a man lost a sheep (see Luke 15:4–6). When he realized it was gone, he left the rest of the flock and searched until he found the one lost sheep. Jesus applied the parable by saying,

> I tell you that in the same way, there will be more joy in heaven over the one sinner who repents, than over the ninety-nine righteous persons who need no repentance.   —*Luke 15:7*

The point of the parable was clear. And it flew right in the face of the Pharisees' twisted theology. God (the shepherd) was concerned about the sinner more than He was the righteous man! But how could that be? Why would He have such concern over sinners when they, the Pharisees, had so faithfully sought to abide by even the most detailed portions of the law? Didn't their righteousness merit God's attention over the unrighteousness of sinners? It didn't make any sense to them at all.

Before they had time to sort it all out, Jesus presented a second scenario. A woman lost a valuable coin, and she put aside all her other household chores until she found it (see Luke 15:8–10). Even at the risk of appearing irresponsible, she searched until she discovered her prize. Again Christ applied the parable to God the Father's attitude toward sinners. In spite of what the religious leaders thought and taught, God's concern at that time was not the righteous but the unrighteous. The source of His joy was not the righteous deeds of the godly but the restoration of the sinner.

The Pharisees would have ended the parables differently. The shepherd wouldn't have gone out of his way to find the missing sheep. Instead he would have written the sheep off as lost for good, no longer a part of the flock. Their attitude would have been, "That sheep knows where to find us. If it wants to rejoin the flock, fine. But it will

Think About It

*The authors
of the New Testament left us
with detailed explanations
of how one becomes a child
of God; if that process could be
reversed, doesn't it make sense
that at least one of them
would have gone into
equal detail explaining
that as well?*

have to come to us. Besides, it should have known better than to wander off."

In the same vein, the woman who lost her coin would have been content with the coins she hadn't lost. She certainly wouldn't be pictured diligently searching for it. After all, it was just *one* coin.

The Pharisees had no comprehension of God's true view of sinners. They were so caught up in their own pseudorighteousness that they had come to believe their good works were actually the grounds for their acceptability before God. To put it in more modern terms, *they believed their salvation was maintained by their good works.*

The Lost Son

To drive His point home even further, Christ gave one more vivid illustration:

> A certain man had two sons; and the younger of them said to his father, "Father, give me the share of the estate that falls to me."
> —*Luke 15:11–12*

With those words Jesus had His audience's undivided attention. From what we understand of first-century Jewish culture, no son with any respect at all for his father would dare demand his share of the inheritance. It was customary for the father to choose the time for the division of the inheritance. To make things worse, the younger son was making the request. What he did was unthinkable!

Jesus continued,

> And he divided his wealth between them. And not many days later, the younger son gathered everything together and went on a journey into a distant country, and there he squandered his estate with loose living. —*Luke 15:12–13*

Not only did he demand his share of the inheritance, the younger son left town with it. Apparently, he had no concern for his father's welfare. He was concerned about only himself. So he took the money, went to a distant country, and partied it all away.

No doubt Jesus' listeners were all rehearsing in their minds what they thought the disrespectful brat deserved. How dare he take such a large portion of his father's hard-earned estate and throw it away! According to the law, a son who cursed his father or was rebellious and stubborn was to be put to death (see Lev. 20:9; Deut. 21:18–21). The death penalty was the most likely verdict reached by many who listened that day.

But then the story took a surprising turn:

> Now when he had spent everything, a severe famine occurred in that country, and he began to be in need. And he went and attached himself to one of the citizens of that country, and he sent him into his fields to feed swine. And he was longing to fill his stomach with the pods that the swine were eating, and no one was giving anything to him. —*Luke 15:14–16*

The crowd must have become almost nauseous as Jesus described the condition in which the boy found himself. The Pharisees would not even go near swine, much less feed them. By their definition, the young man was hopelessly ceremonially unclean. That is, he would probably never get clean enough to enter the temple and offer sacrifices. And to think he would even consider eating with the pigs. To them, he had gone over the edge, but then, he deserved it.

At the same time, however, many who stood there that day could relate to the story of the prodigal son. They had abandoned their heavenly Father. Like the lad in the story, they were in situations that caused them to be alienated from the religious community. By the practiced standard of the day, they were unacceptable to God. They listened carefully as Jesus went on,

> But when he came to his senses, he said, "How many of my father's hired men have more than enough bread, but I am dying

here with hunger! I will get up and go to my father, and will say to him, 'Father, I have sinned against heaven, and in your sight; I am no longer worthy to be called your son; make me as one of your hired men.' " And he got up and came to his father.
                                            —*Luke 15:17-20*

I imagine everyone who heard Jesus that day had an opinion about what the father should say or do when the boy began his speech. At the same time, I doubt any of them would have ended the parable the way Jesus did:

But while he was still a long way off, his father saw him, and felt compassion for him, and ran and embraced him, and kissed him.
                                            —*Luke 15:20*

The Pharisees must have cringed at the thought of embracing someone who had spent time feeding swine. Jesus then added,

And the son said to him, "Father, I have sinned against heaven and in your sight; I am no longer worthy to be called your son." But the father said to his slaves, "Quickly bring out the best robe and put it on him, and put a ring on his hand and sandals on his feet; and bring the fattened calf, kill it, and let us eat and be merry; for this son of mine was dead, and has come to life again; he was lost, and has been found."   —*Luke 15:21-24*

A Worst Case Scenario

Culturally speaking, what Jesus described in the parable was a worst case scenario. The boy could not have been more disrespectful. He could not have been any more insensitive. And he certainly could not have been a greater embarrassment to the family.

No one would have blamed the father if he had refused to allow the boy to join up as one of his hired men. The son didn't deserve a second chance, and he knew it. He recognized how foolish it would be to return with the notion of being allowed back into the family. That was not even a consideration. *In his mind, he had forfeited all*

51

rights to sonship. He was of the conviction that by abandoning his father and wasting his inheritance, he had relinquished his position in the family.

Once a Son, Always a Son

His father, however, did not see things that way at all. In his mind, *once a son, always a son.* The father's first emotion as he saw the son returning wasn't anger. It wasn't even disappointment. He felt *compassion* for him. Why? Because the young man was his son!

The father said: "This son of mine was dead and has come to life again" (Luke 15:24). He did not say, "This was my son, and now he is my son again." On the contrary, there is no hint that the *relationship* was ever broken, only the *fellowship.* By "dead" Jesus meant "separated." That was clearly a figure of speech since the son did not physically die in the parable.

Christ's next words have been used by some to argue that salvation can be lost. He went on to say, "He was lost, and has been found" (v. 24). To say that "lost" and "found" refer to eternal salvation is to assume that they are being used figuratively. But there is no evidence for such a use from the immediate context. The son was literally *lost.* That is, the father did not know where he was. When the son returned, he was *found.*

A Missed Opportunity

Since the point of the three parables was to illustrate God's attitude toward sinners, Christ had the perfect opportunity to explain how one could lose his or her place in the family of God—if such were possible. That is especially true when we think about the characters in the third parable. The parallels are too obvious to miss. The father is the heavenly Father, and the son represents sinners of all kinds.

If ever there was a son who deserved to be disowned, it was the son in the parable. If ever there was a set of circumstances within a family that called for extreme action, that was it. Yet there was no hint of rejection on the part of the Heavenly Father. The father in the story was not portrayed as one battling in his heart over what to do with his sorry son.

Jesus did not depict the heavenly Father as One waiting to be asked for permission to reenter the family. Instead He was described as One who felt compassion for the returning sinner, One who at no time viewed the son as anything less than that—a son. He was pictured as One who took immediate action to restore His wandering child to a place of honor and dignity. He demanded no explanation; no apology; nothing. There was no probationary period, just acceptance and joy.

What Is the Connection?

To those who believe salvation is maintained by good works, I would ask, What good works maintained the relationship between the father and the son in the parable? It is clear that he left as a son; otherwise he would have received no inheritance. It is equally clear that he returned as a son. Without a word between them, the father ran to him, embraced him, and restored to him the visible signs of sonship.

What maintained the son's relationship with the father? He certainly wasn't acting like a son. He didn't manifest any signs of sonship. He didn't perform good works. If anything, his life-style was characterized by the very opposite! Yet his relationship with the father never changed. Why? Because the father's love and acceptance of the son were not contingent on the son's works. The father's love was unconditional. He loved the son because he was a son, because they were related.

That was Jesus' point exactly. The shepherd didn't kick

the wandering sheep out of the flock. The woman didn't just forget about her lost coin and turn her attention to ones she still possessed. And the prodigal's father didn't disown his rebellious son. In every case, the opposite was true.

God is not looking for people He can throw out of His family. He is looking for people who are willing to be included. And once they are included by faith, He continually looks after them through all their ups and downs. He is the Good Shepherd, the compassionate Father. He is love.

If you have placed your trust in Christ's death on the cross as the payment for your sin, you are an eternal member of the family of God. Acting like God's child didn't get you in. Not acting like one won't get you tossed out. God's unconditional love is eternal. Salvation is forever.

Notes

1. It is interesting to note that the Pharisee's security was wrapped up in his ability to keep the law. Jesus said he was trusting in himself for his security (see Luke 18:9). But isn't it true that people who believe they must maintain some kind of good works in order to *stay saved* are trusting in themselves for their eternal security? They can talk all they want about how they must depend on the power of God within them to walk the Christian walk. But the bottom line is that they *choose* to live a godly life; therefore, they are ultimately responsible for maintaining their salvation. If that is the case, we are saved by faith and kept by works. Thus, salvation is not a *gift;* it is merely an *opportunity.*

Do You Know?

1. *How did the religious leaders of Jesus' day believe righteousness was gained and maintained?*
2. *What did Jesus' eating with sinners symbolize?*
3. *In the parable of the prodigal son, are the terms* lost *and* found *used literally or figuratively?*
4. *How does the parable of the prodigal son disprove the notion of salvation by good works?*

6

Signed, Sealed, and Delivered

Every husband has experienced the frustration and embarrassment of offering to help his wife open a new jar or bottle only to find that for all his strength and good intentions, the top wouldn't budge! With a look of defeat we grudgingly turn the project back over to our wives. On comes the hot water. And in a few seconds the seal is broken and the top comes right off. We slip back into the den, pretending like the whole event never took place.

Despite its potential threat to our masculinity, there is something comforting about hearing a seal pop open. It assures us that nothing inside the jar has been tampered with. We can be certain that the contents have been protected, regardless of where the container has been or who handled it last.

On a much grander scale, there is a seal assuring each believer that no one has tampered with his or her eternal security. Paul said it this way:

> In Him, you also, after listening to the message of truth, the gospel of your salvation—having also believed, you were *sealed* in Him with the Holy Spirit of promise, who is given as a pledge of our inheritance, with a view to the redemption of God's own possession, to the praise of His glory.
> —*Ephesians 1:13–14, emphasis mine*

Various Uses

The term *sealed* is used various ways in the New Testament. In Matthew 27:66 we read that Jesus' tomb was *sealed* by the Romans. In Revelation we are told that Satan will be *sealed* in the abyss for one thousand years. There are several references to books that were *sealed* (see Rev. 6). We read that during the Tribulation God will place a *seal* on 144,000 people from the tribe of Israel (see Rev. 7).

In every case the term *sealed* carried with it the ideas of protection and security. To seal something, whether it was a document or a tomb, was to close it off from outside influences and interferences.

That is still true today. We seal windows and doors to keep the wind out. We seal letters to keep everyone out except the addressee. We seal our basements to keep water out. We even put a seal on our furniture to keep the dust from getting into the pores of the wood.

The Divine Seal of Approval

As a believer, you have been sealed. We know this to be true because in his second letter to the Corinthians Paul does not qualify in any way this statement:

> Now He who establishes us with you in Christ and anointed us is God, who also sealed us and gave us the Spirit in our hearts as a pledge.   *—2 Corinthians 1:21–22*

As one writer put it,

> Sealing belongs to believers only and to all believers. In 2 Corinthians 1:22 Paul makes no exceptions in writing to a group in which exceptions could easily be justified.[1]

You have been sealed. The moment you trusted Christ as your Savior, God sealed you. In light of the varied uses of this term, several questions must be addressed. First of all, what is the nature of this seal? Are we sealed like a letter? Are we sealed like a tomb? Second, what is the purpose of our sealing? And third, how long are we sealed?

A Fitting Illustration

In our culture we do not usually think of putting a seal on people. Therefore, it is a bit difficult to imagine the significance of being sealed by God. Fortunately, we have an illustration in Scripture that clarifies this matter for us.

During the Tribulation, God will place a seal on 144,000 Jews (see Rev. 7:4–8). The seal is apparently some sort of visible mark on the forehead. As the Tribulation progresses, it becomes evident that the members of this group bearing God's seal have been granted supernatural protection from the chaos surrounding them. At the end of the Tribulation period, the entire group reappears intact to welcome the King (see Rev. 14:1–5).

This powerful illustration helps us understand the ramifications of God's placing His seal on an individual. The primary benefit of the seal is clearly that of protection. The seal protects this group during the most dangerous period in the history of mankind. Nothing is able to overcome the power of this seal, not even the Antichrist himself!

Unlike the 144,000 mentioned in Revelation, our seal is not visible. We have been sealed "in Him." Our seal is spiritual, not physical. Instead of receiving a mark on our foreheads, we were given the Holy Spirit as a pledge of God's intent to preserve us:

> Now He who establishes us with you in Christ and anointed us is God, who also sealed us and *gave us the Spirit in our hearts as a pledge.* —*2 Corinthians 1:21–22, emphasis mine*

The Holy Spirit is a *pledge* of God's intentions. He is not finished with us yet. But the presence of the Spirit demonstrates God's commitment to complete what He has started. If salvation is not permanent, God is simply playing games by sending the Spirit into our hearts. It would

Think About It

*What is the significance
of a seal that can be
continually removed
and reapplied?
What does it
really seal?*

be like a man's giving a woman an engagement ring when he knows he has no intention of marrying her.

A Divine Purpose

The device used to indicate God's seal in our lives is certainly different from the one He chose for the 144,000. His purpose for sealing us, however, is the same. Just as their physical seal protected them from losing physical life, so our spiritual seal ensures the longevity of spiritual life. Just as the physical forces of evil could not take away the physical life of those Jews who bore the seal, so, too, the spiritual forces of darkness cannot put an end to the spiritual life of God's people.

How Long?

As long as the 144,000 bear the seal, they will be safe. As long as we are sealed in Him, we are safe as well. That brings us to our third question: How long does the seal last? Once again God has been gracious to give us an answer through the apostle Paul:

> And do not grieve the Holy Spirit of God, by whom you were sealed for the day of redemption.   —*Ephesians 4:30*

We are sealed right up through the "day of redemption." The day of redemption refers to that day when our salvation will be complete—body and spirit. As it is stated in the book of Romans,

> We ourselves groan within ourselves, waiting eagerly for our adoption as sons, the redemption of our body.
> —*Romans 8:23*

Our salvation will not be complete until we receive our new bodies:

> For this perishable must put on the imperishable, and this mortal must put on immortality. —*1 Corinthians 15:53*

There are no exceptions. Everyone who has been sealed in Christ will remain sealed right up through the end. Peter echoes this thought in his first epistle. He points out that each believer has an inheritance reserved in heaven. Believers, he says,

> are protected by the power of God through faith for a salvation ready to be revealed *in the last time.*
> —*1 Peter 1:5, emphasis mine*

Again, we find that our salvation will not be complete until the end of time. But until then, we are protected by "the power of God."

No Way Out

Only God can break the seal (see Rev. 5:1–3). And the Scriptures clearly teach that He has already determined to leave the seal intact until our salvation is complete. How, then, could we possibly lose our salvation? To be unsaved would mean to remove the seal. Who could possibly do that?

For those who maintain that salvation is not forever, this question poses an insurmountable obstacle. For those who believe otherwise, it leaves us with unquestionable certainty.

Notes

1. Charles C. Ryrie, *Basic Theology* (Wheaton, Ill.: Victor Books, 1987), p. 359.

Do You Know?

1. *As it is used in Scripture, what does the term* sealed *imply?*
2. *How does the "spiritual seal" protect God's people? How long does the seal last?*
3. *When is our salvation complete?*
4. *Why can't salvation be lost if God has sealed His people?*

7

Who Will Perish?

Eternal damnation is undoubtedly one of the most difficult, if not *the* most difficult, teachings of the Christian
faith. How can God justify punishing a man or woman
eternally for sins committed over a period of a few years?
It doesn't seem right. Yet the Scriptures definitely teach
that hell is a real place for real people:

> And the devil who deceived them was thrown into the lake of fire
> and brimstone, where the beast and the false prophet are also;
> and they will be tormented day and night forever and ever. . . .
> And if anyone's name was not found written in the book of life,
> he was thrown into the lake of fire. —*Revelation 20:10, 15*

The purpose of this chapter is to ascertain why some
people will spend eternity in hell, why certain people's
names will not show up in the book of life as described in
Revelation 20. What separates those who will spend eternity in hell from those who will not?

This question is important in light of our topic. According to those who believe you can lose your salvation,
*whatever it is that sends a person to hell can be done and
undone repeatedly.* Thus the names written in the book of
life can be erased and rewritten again and again. This
view is supported with texts such as Revelation 3:5 and
Psalm 69:28. We will deal with these passages later. But for
now, what sends someone to hell?

Both sides agree on two things: (1) all men have sinned
(see Rom. 3:23), and (2) yet some of these sinners will

make it to heaven (see 2 Cor. 5:6–8). Obviously, sin is not the only reason people spend eternity in hell. There is a category of sinners who escape eternal punishment. What separates them from the rest?

Severity of Sin?

No doubt you have met someone who has a particular sin in his or her background that the person feels is too severe for God to forgive. One young man expressed his feelings this way: "I know God is forgiving, but He's not blind." That was his way of saying, "Sure, God can forgive some things, but look what I've done." In the minds of many, there are certain sins so grave that God either cannot or will not forgive them. Consequently, those who have involved themselves in these particular actions are destined for hell.

If that were the case, surely God would have led someone to record for us in the Bible a list of the unpardonable sins.[1] A loving God would not leave us to guess about such a vital issue. But that kind of list does not exist. In Paul's first letter to the Corinthians, we find the very opposite to be true:

> Neither fornicators, nor idolaters, nor adulterers, nor effeminate, nor homosexuals, nor thieves, nor the covetous, nor drunkards, nor revilers, nor swindlers, shall inherit the kingdom of God. And such *were* some of you; but you were washed, but you were sanctified, but you were justified in the name of the Lord Jesus Christ, and in the Spirit of our God.
> —*1 Corinthians 6:9–11, emphasis mine*

People guilty of all manner of sexual and unethical sins had found forgiveness through Christ. And the author himself was guilty of persecuting the church and dragging Christians off to prison. Hell is not reserved for those who commit certain types of sin. Otherwise Paul could not have said what he did to the believers in Corinth.

If there are sins so severe that they determine a man's fate, certainly the murder of the Son of God would be one. What greater crime could be committed in the whole of human history? Yet, in the gospel of Luke we read that Jesus looked down on the very people who were crucifying Him and said,

> Father, forgive them; for they do not know what they are doing.
> —*Luke 23:34*

As strange as it may sound, killing the Son of God was not severe enough to put those men outside the boundaries of God's offer of forgiveness.

Repetition of Sin?

"But," someone asks, "what about a man who keeps repeating the same sin over and over again? Surely God grows weary; eventually even *His* patience must run out. Even if he repents after each offense, soon it becomes apparent that the man's repentance is insincere." Is this the type of person destined for hell?

Again, the answer is no. Jesus dealt specifically with this issue in a dialogue with the disciples. He said,

> Be on your guard! If your brother sins, rebuke him; and if he repents, forgive him. And if he sins against you seven times a day, and returns to you seven times, saying, "I repent," forgive him.
> —*Luke 17:3-4*

Jesus went to an unreal extreme to make a simple, yet difficult to accept, point. The Son of God taught that if someone sins against us seven times a day, we are to forgive him. His point was not that we are to limit ourselves to seven times, but that we are to continually forgive others regardless of how often they offend us or how insincere their apology may be.

Think About It

If a man or a woman
ends up in hell, who has
at some point in life
put his or her trust in Christ,
doesn't that make what
Jesus said to Nicodemus a lie?
Or at best
only half true?

Unbelief

What, then, sends a person to hell? What guarantees the omission of a man's or woman's name from the book of life? What is the ingredient that, mixed with sin, somehow ensures one's condemnation to the lake of fire? Sinning alone will not do, for as we have seen, sinners of every description have the potential for escaping hell.

The clearest teaching on this subject is conveyed in the conversation between Jesus and Nicodemus. It is a passage that contains what may be the most familiar verse in the entire New Testament:

> For God so loved the world, that He gave His only begotten Son, that whoever believes in Him should not perish, but have eternal life. For God did not send the Son into the world to judge the world, but that the world should be saved through Him.
> —*John 3:16–17*

What keeps a man from perishing? Jesus did not cite for Nicodemus a list of sins and then add, "As long as a man keeps himself from these, he will not perish." His only condition was belief in Him.

Notice His next words:

> He who believes in Him is not judged; he who does not believe has been judged already, because he has not believed in the name of the only begotten Son of God.   —*John 3:18*

Look at that verse and answer this question: According to Jesus, what must a person do to keep from being judged for sin? Must he stop doing something? Must he promise to stop doing something? Must he have never done something? The answer is so simple that many stumble all over it without ever seeing it. All Jesus requires is that the individual "believe in" Him.

Look again. What is true of someone who has already been judged? Did he commit an unpardonable sin of

67

some sort? No! He is judged because he has "not believed in" the Son of God.

Escaping Judgment

Now we have to consider two questions. First, what kind of judgment is Christ referring to? Clearly He does not mean the judgment seat of Christ, for Paul said that "we must all" appear there for judgment (see 2 Cor. 5:10). Apparently, not *all* of us will be judged in the sense that Christ is referring to here.

Second, Jesus implies that some men who are still alive have already been judged. Men do not stand before the judgment seat of Christ until after they have died. Otherwise they would not be able to give an account of their lives. Jesus had something else in mind other than the judgment seat.

He cannot be referring to the Great White Throne Judgment because this judgment is reserved for men and women after life on this earth has ended (see Rev. 20:11–15). Furthermore, this event is described in Revelation as a one-time occurrence. The type of judgment Jesus speaks of in John is an ongoing thing. Some men will not be judged; some have been judged; others are being judged. What kind of judgment is He talking about here?

Jesus tells us:

And this is the judgment, that the light is come into the world, and men loved the darkness rather than the light; for their deeds were evil.   *—John 3:19*

Jesus uses the term *judgment* to refer to the condemnation that comes as a result of refusing to turn to Christ for salvation. By refusing to "believe in" Christ, people condemn themselves! Jesus is not condemning them. At that particular time in history as well as in this present age, He was and is serving as Savior, not Judge (see John 3:17).

But when people turn away from the Savior, they have brought condemnation upon themselves.

One writer offered these insights:

> In a gallery where artistic masterpieces are on display, it is not the masterpieces but the visitors who are on trial. . . . The pop-star who was reported some years ago to have dismissed the Mona Lisa as "a load of rubbish (except that he used a less polite word than 'rubbish')" did not tell us anything about the Mona Lisa; he told us much about himself. What is true in the aesthetic realm is equally true in the spiritual realm. The man who depreciates Christ, or thinks him unworthy of his allegiance, passes judgment on himself, not on Christ. He does not need to wait until the day of judgment; the verdict on him has been pronounced already. There will indeed be a final day of judgment (John 5:25–29), but that day will serve only to confirm the judgment already passed.[2]

"He Who Believes"

Another question raised by Jesus' dialogue with Nicodemus is this: What does it mean to "believe in" Jesus? The term *believe* can have several connotations. Someone may say, "I believe it will rain this afternoon." In that case it carries the idea of "calculated hope." Oftentimes I hear people declare, "I believe in God." Here *believe* denotes "mental assent to an idea," that is, the existence of God. There is no sense of trust or commitment in such a statement, just the acceptance of an idea.

John had neither of these uses of *believe* in mind when he wrote, "He who believes in Him is not judged." *To believe in* Jesus in the sense that John intended in that phrase means "to trust in" Him.

Webster's Third New International Dictionary defines *trust* as "assured reliance on some person or thing: a confident dependence on the character, ability, strength, or truth of someone or something." Trust denotes personal involvement. It assumes a relationship of some kind. The difference between belief and trust is illustrated in the difference between my acknowledging a bridge can hold me up and my actually walking out onto the bridge. The former is no more than calculated hope or mental assent to what I have been told. The latter, however, is a demonstration of dependence.

As was pointed out in chapter 3, the biblical support for this idea comes from a grammatical construct that occurs repeatedly where faith is mentioned in connection with forgiveness and salvation. This construct consists of the Greek word that means "believe" followed by a little word translated "in" or "on," depending on the context of the passage. The combination of the term for "believe" and this little preposition is unique to the New Testament.

Putting It Together

How does all this relate to the subject of eternal security? The debate is over whether or not a man can be on his way to heaven one minute and on his way to hell the next. To answer that question, we must understand exactly what sends a person to hell. As we have seen, sin alone is not enough. Heaven will be full of people who committed all kinds of sin. It takes more than simply sinning to get to hell.

Jesus gives us the rest of the equation in John 3. Sinners who do not put their trust in Christ perish and miss eternal life. In fact, sinners who reject Christ have done it to themselves; they are as good as there! They would have nothing to do with Christ in this life, and so they will have nothing to do with Him for eternity. It is not lying, cheating, stealing, raping, murdering, or being unfaithful that sends people to hell. It is rejecting Christ, refusing to put their trust in Him for the forgiveness of sin.

There are many similarities between salvation and marriage. A person does not become married by acting married. Neither does one gain a divorce by acting divorced. A man and woman are married by entering into a legal contract. Obtaining a divorce is a legal matter as well. Whether they ever *act* married or not is irrelevant. I have known several couples who separated and adopted life-styles that gave no evidence of their marital status. Yet they were as married then as the day they said their vows.

In the same way, we don't become saved by acting saved. Neither do we become unsaved by acting unsaved. Salvation, as we have seen, occurs at a moment in time when we by faith accept God's free gift. At that point in time God declares us "not guilty."

Just as there are married people who act as if they are not, so there are Christians who show no evidence of their Christianity as well. But that does not change their eternal status, any more than a lost man can change his eternal destiny by acting saved.

But What About . . .

I can hear the pages of the skeptic's Bible turning as he rushes to point out other passages of Scripture that appear to teach something different or should I say "balance" what I have said thus far. And we will deal with many of those verses in later chapters. But for now, do not lose sight of one extremely important point: Nicodemus had no other New Testament Scripture. And it is clear from his dialogue with Jesus that his grasp of the Old Testament was not all it should have been! Did Jesus shoot straight with Nic? Was there something He forgot to tell him? Did He leave him with only half the truth? Did He assume Nicodemus would one day pick up a copy of Galatians or Hebrews to complete his theology? I think not.

Jesus' message was simple. Eternal life is found through faith and faith alone. Both heaven and hell will be full of men and women who have committed every imaginable evil. The difference is not in the severity of their sin, or in the number of their offenses, but in their response to the offer of the Savior.

Notes

1. We will deal with *the* unpardonable sin in a later chapter.
2. F. F. Bruce, *The Gospel of John* (Grand Rapids, Mich.: Eerdmans, 1983), p. 91.

Do You Know?

1. *If all people are sinners—including Christians—why is it that some people escape hell?*
2. *Are there some sins so severe that the door to heaven is barred to anyone who commits them?*
3. *Is the person who keeps repeating the same sin over and over again destined for hell?*
4. *According to the author, what is Jesus referring to when he uses the term* judgment?
5. *What is the difference in concept between the terms* believe *and* believe in?

8

For Those Who Stop Believing

People on both sides of this issue agree for the most part that we are saved by faith. However, those who believe salvation can be lost often ask an insightful question about the relationship between salvation and faith. That question can be phrased,

> If our salvation is gained through believing in Christ, doesn't it make sense that salvation would be lost if we quit believing?

Or to put it another way,

> If Christians lose faith to the point that they no longer recognize Christ's death on the cross as the payment for sin, doesn't it follow that they would lose their salvation as well?

Or to put it in a scriptural context,

> John 6:47 says, "He who believes has eternal life." Does it not follow then that he who does not believe does not have eternal life?

Along the same lines, some have argued that the term *believe,* when referring to salvation, is always used in the present tense, as is the case in John 6:47. The implication is that a believer is one who is *always* believing. Therefore, to stop believing is to disqualify oneself from the family of believers.[1]

As convincing as these arguments may sound, they are

73

shot through with problems. The Bible clearly teaches that God's love for His people is of such magnitude that even those who walk away from the faith have not the slightest chance of slipping from His hand.

Faith and Salvation

Let's begin with a fundamental question: What does the Bible say about the relationship between believing and salvation? We have already seen that faith is a key ingredient in gaining salvation. But let's go beyond that. Let's focus on the specific connection between the two. The apostle Paul explains their association this way:

> But God, being rich in mercy, because of His great love with which He loved us, even when we were dead in our transgressions, made us alive together with Christ (by grace you have been saved), and raised us up with Him, and seated us with Him in the heavenly places, in Christ Jesus, in order that in the ages to come He might show the surpassing riches of His grace in kindness toward us in Christ Jesus. For by grace you have been saved through faith; and that not of yourselves, it is the gift of God; not as a result of works, that no one should boast.
> —*Ephesians 2:4–9*

At the very outset Paul makes an important theological point. The reason ("because of . . .") God made us alive was His "great love." Why is that so important? Because right up front we discover the reason or motivation behind our salvation. Paul does not say, "Because of our great abiding faith with which we trusted Him." *Faith* is not the reason God saves men. *Love* is the reason.

The Motivation of God's Salvation

We did nothing to motivate God to save us. His motivation was intrinsic. It came from within His nature. He saw our plight and felt compassion for us. Anyone who has stopped along the road to pick up a stray dog or move a

74

fallen bird's nest to a safe place has in a limited way mir-
rored the compassion expressed by God in salvation.

Paul explains this even further with his parenthetical
remark, "By grace you have been saved." The Greek form
of the term *grace* implies that grace is the "instrument"
used to accomplish salvation.[2] In other words, if one were
to ask God, "God, how did You save me?" He would answer, "Grace."

Grace summarizes the entire salvation process. It en-
capsulates the sending of Christ, the offer of forgiveness,
His crucifixion, His resurrection, and His ascension. Why
grace? Because grace indicates unmerited favor; it suggests an undeserved expression of kindness and goodwill.
The whole of salvation is just that—an undeserved gift.
From start to finish, salvation is by grace. We have now
answered two basic questions.

Q1: Why did God save us?
A1: He loved us.

Q2: How did God save us?
A2: By grace; by an undeserved series of events en-
acted for our benefit.

God's Purpose

Paul answers yet another crucial question. In verse 7 he
reveals the *purpose* for our salvation:[3] so that we might be
the eternal objects of God's kindness.

This truth underscores the depth of the love that moved
God to begin with. Unlike the nature lover who stops to
rescue an injured bird, God's love goes beyond pity. He
did not save us just to keep us out of hell. He saved us to
guarantee an eternal relationship with us, a relationship in
which we would continue to be the recipients of His kindness.

God's grace toward you did not stop with forgiveness.

Think About It

*Is there anything keeping you
from accepting
God's free gift
of salvation
right now?*

His grace will continue to be poured out on you forever! That was His purpose from the very beginning.

Before we go any further, you need to ask yourself a sobering question: "Do I believe I have the power to thwart the purposes of God?" Once God has made up His mind He is going to do something, do you think you have the power to throw a wrench into the works and foul things up? To believe that a man or woman can lose his or her salvation is to believe that a human being can frustrate the eternal purpose of God.

God has plans for all those who were dead in their trespasses and sins and have been made alive with Christ. To hold to a theology in which man can do something that throws him back into a state of spiritual deadness, thus denying God His predetermined purpose, is to embrace a system in which man is in the driver's seat and God is just a passenger.[4]

. . . By Faith

At last we come to the focus of our discussion—the relationship between faith and salvation. Whether you are aware of it or not, we have eliminated several commonly accepted views about faith and salvation. First of all, we have learned that *faith is not the reason God saves us.* Remember, Paul makes it clear that love is the reason.

Second, *we are not saved* by *our faith.* We are saved by grace. The instrument of salvation was and is grace. God came up with a plan and carried it out through Christ. We did not take part in it, nor did we deserve any part of it. It was grace from start to finish. "How then," you are asking, "does faith fit in with all of this?" Paul clarifies that by saying,

> For by grace you have been saved through faith; and that not of yourselves, it is the gift of God; not as a result of works, that no one should boast.   —*Ephesians 2:8–9*

Once again Paul explains the role of grace. But then he adds the ever-so-important—yet misunderstood—phrase "through faith." "Through" is the key to understanding the significance of faith. "Through" is translated from the Greek word *dia,* which carries the idea of "means" or "agency."[5] Faith was the agent whereby God was able to apply His grace to the life of the sinner.

A parallel use of the term is found in Paul's first letter to the Corinthians:

> For since in the wisdom of God the world through its wisdom did not come to know God, God was well-pleased *through* the foolishness of the message preached to save those who believe.
> —*1 Corinthians 1:21, emphasis mine*

The message was the agent through which salvation was made available to the group of people in question. Paul is not saying that the message itself saved them. The message was simply the means by which the saving grace of God was explained.

A Desperate Leap

Imagine for a moment that you are at the scene of a burning building. You notice a crowd of people shouting and pointing up at one end of the building, so you run to see what all the commotion is about. When you arrive, you are told by firemen that a woman is trapped on a ledge three floors up. Her only hope is to jump into the net that has been set up right below her.

As you peer through the smoke, you finally catch a glimpse of the woman. She is obviously scared and confused. You see the net not too far from where you are standing. It certainly looks strong enough to hold the woman, and apparently, the firemen are confident that if she will simply jump, her life will be spared.

Suddenly, without warning the woman screams and

leaps from the building. The firemen brace themselves to help absorb the impact of the woman's body as she hits the safety net. As the sides of the net are lowered, you see that the woman escaped with only minor injuries. The crowd cheers, and you go on your merry way.

Now, think for a moment. What saved the woman's life?

The net, of course. No one would credit her with saving her own life. Fortunately for her, trained firemen were on the spot who knew how to handle emergency situations. They formulated a plan, went to work on it, and carried it out.

But what bridged the gap between her need and the provision waiting below? One desperate leap! However, leaping did not save her. Many people have jumped from burning buildings only to end up dead on the pavement below. The net and the firemen saved her.

So it is with faith. Faith does not save a person. Everybody has expressed faith at some point or another. Yet not everyone will spend eternity in heaven. God's grace is what saves us. *Our faith, however, is the thing that bridges the gap between our need and God's provision;* specifically, it is a point in time at which the expression of faith in Christ brings God's provision together with our need. Once the woman jumped, she was safe. Once we believe, we are saved.

I imagine a woman who went through an experience such as the one described would always have faith in firemen and their nets. But even if she did not, the fact remains that she was saved from the fire. In the same way, in all probability, a Christian who has expressed faith in Christ and experienced forgiveness of sin will always believe that forgiveness is found through Christ. But even if he does not, the fact remains that he is forgiven!

It is true that the same woman could find herself caught in a different fire. And it is equally true that the degeneration of her faith in firemen and their nets could be deadly. But a man or woman who has been rescued once from a state of unforgiveness need not worry. For once 100 percent of a man's or woman's sins have been forgiven, the potential for being unforgiven has been done away with. The risk factor is zero. There are no more fires from which the believer needs to be saved.

Yes!

Faith is simply the way we say yes to God's free gift of eternal life. Faith and salvation are not one and the same anymore than a gift and the hand that receives it are the same. Salvation or justification or adoption—whatever you wish to call it—stands independently of faith. Consequently, God does not require a *constant attitude* of faith in order to be saved—only an *act* of faith.

One more illustration may be helpful. If I chose to have a tattoo put on my arm, that would involve a one-time act on my part. Yet the tattoo would remain with me indefinitely. I don't have to maintain an attitude of fondness for tattoos to ensure that the tattoo remains on my arm. In fact I may change my mind the minute I receive it. But that does not change the fact that I have a tattoo on my arm. My request for the tattoo and the tattoo itself are two entirely different things. I received it by asking and paying for it. But asking for my money back and changing my attitude will not undo what is done.

Forgiveness/salvation is applied at the moment of faith. It is not the same thing as faith. And its permanence is not contingent upon the permanence of one's faith.

A Gift Is a Gift Is a Gift

You and I are not saved because we have enduring faith. We are saved because at a moment in time we expressed faith in our enduring Lord. Notice how Paul ends this passage:

It is the gift of God; not as a result of works, that no one should boast.
—*Ephesians 2:8–9*

Pictured here is something we experience every time we are handed a gift. *It* refers to the entire process Paul has just finished describing, that is, salvation.[6] "Salvation," Paul says, "is a gift." Now I don't know about you, but I have learned that a gift that can be taken back is no gift. True gifts have no strings attached. Once you place a condition of any kind on a gift, it becomes a trade, not a gift.

To say that our salvation can be taken from us for any reason, whether it be sin or disbelief, is to ignore the plain meaning of this text. To place conditions on the permanency of our salvation is to say it is not a gift. Therefore, placing conditions on the permanency of salvation is the equivalent of not believing Ephesians 2:8 or John 4:10 or other passages where salvation is clearly described as a gift.

What we do with the gift is another matter entirely. The fact that I don't take advantage of a gift says nothing about who it belongs to. It still belongs to me. You can take a gift and bury it in the back yard, but it is still yours. Once you accept a gift, you are stuck with it, like it or not!

You say, "What if I give it back?" You can give it back only if the giver accepts the return. In the case of salvation God has a strict no-return policy. There is no evidence by way of statement or illustration that God has ever taken back from a believer the gift of salvation once it has been given. His love would keep Him from doing so. Keep in mind, Christ came to seek and to save the lost. Why would He take back what He came to give?

And faith? Faith is our way of accepting God's gift. Faith serves as our spiritual hands by which the gift is received at a particular moment in time. Again, saving faith is not necessarily a sustained attitude of gratefulness for God's gift. It is a singular moment in time wherein we take what God has offered.

Before we go any further, let me ask you this: Has there been a time in your life when you accepted God's free gift of salvation? If not, why not settle the issue once and for all right now? It's really so simple. God is not looking for a series of promises. His primary concern at this point is not your ability to follow through. He does not want to hear all the things you intend to do for Him. He is more concerned about what you will let Him do for you.

When I was twelve, I prayed a prayer similar to the one I've included here. If you are not sure you are saved, why not make sure now? If you recognize your need for forgiveness and you believe Christ's death made your forgiveness possible, you are ready. Pray,

God,
I know I am a sinner.
I know my sin has earned for me eternal separation from You.
I believe Christ died in my place when He died at Calvary.
I accept His death as the full payment for my sin.
I accept Him as my Savior.
Thank You for saving me.
In Jesus' name I pray.
Amen.

Notes

1. Robert Shank uses this line of reasoning to argue against the eternal security of the believer in *Life in the Son* (Springfield, Mo.: Wescott, 1960).
2. C. F. D. Moule, *An Idiom Book of New Testament Greek* (New York: Cambridge University Press, 1959), p. 44.
3. "In order that" translates *hina*. This Greek conjunction is almost always used to signify the idea of either purpose or result. Since what is spoken of here is still in the future, purpose seems to fit best.
4. This view does not jeopardize man's freedom. Experientially, man is free to choose or reject God's gift of salvation. However, to reject salvation in no way thwarts the purposes of God. Nowhere does Scripture teach that God has *purposed* that every man and woman be saved. We must differentiate here between matters of desire and matters of purpose. God desires that every person be saved, but He has not purposed

that it be so. He has purposed, however, that every person who is saved at any point eventually be the object of His grace in the ages to come. To say that man can do something that causes him to lose his salvation is to say he has the ability to block God in carrying out His purposes. If this is in fact the case, all of prophecy is up for grabs, for how can we legitimately make a distinction between the purpose of God as stated in Ephesians and that of Revelation?

5. Bauer, Gingrich, and Danker, *A Greek-English Lexicon of the New Testament and Early Christian Literature,* 2d ed. (Chicago: University of Chicago Press, 1979), p. 180, section III, subsection 1, d.

6. Many argue that *it* refers to faith, and therefore, the gift is faith. Grammatically speaking, that evaluation of what Paul had in mind is doubtful. The pronoun *it* is neuter. *Faith* and *grace* are feminine. The use of a neuter pronoun following these feminine nouns indicates that *it* refers to a broader idea. Paul probably had the entire salvation scenario in mind here. Salvation is a gift. See A. T. A. Robertson, *Grammar of the Greek New Testament* (Nashville: Broadman Press, 1934), p. 704.

Do You Know?

1. *What does the Greek form of the term* grace *imply?*
2. *According to the apostle Paul, what is the* purpose *of our salvation?*
3. *What bridges the gap between our need and God's provision?*
4. *Does God require a person to have a constant attitude of faith in order to be saved? Explain.*
5. *How would you answer the author's question, "Has there been a time in your life when you accepted God's free gift of salvation?"*

9

"He Who Believes . . ."

As noted in the previous chapter, some people argue that the believer must maintain his *faith* in order to maintain his *salvation.* The primary scriptural support for this view comes from the apostle John's use of the present tense in connection with the term *believe,* for example.

> And as Moses lifted up the serpent in the wilderness even so must the Son of Man be lifted up; that whoever *believes* may in Him have eternal life. For God so loved the world, that He gave His only begotten Son, that whoever *believes* in Him should not perish, but have eternal life. *—John 3:14–16, emphasis added; see also 3:18; 5:24; 6::29, 6:40*

Those who subscribe to this argument understand the present tense to denote continuous, uninterrupted action. In other words, they understand John 3:16 to read, "That whoever *keeps on believing* in Him should not perish, but have eternal life." The implication is that "whoever does not keep on believing will not have eternal life" or "will lose eternal life."

Another passage sometimes cited to support this view is found in the book of James:

> But let him ask in faith without any doubting, for the one who doubts is like the surf of the sea driven and tossed by the wind. For let not that man expect that he will receive anything from the Lord, being a double-minded man, unstable in all his ways.
> *—James 1:6–8*

James says that the one who doubts will not receive anything from God. Would this not include salvation as well?

How Present Is Present?

There are several problems with this argument. The first one has to do with their understanding of the present tense. This argument restricts the meaning of the present tense.

If someone were to ask me sometime this week, "Charles, what are you doing in your spare time these days," I might respond, "Well, I'm writing a book and working in my dark room."

In my response I used progressive forms of two present tense verbs, *writing* and *working*. But no one would ascertain from my answer that in my spare time I am writing and working in my dark room at the same time. Neither would the understanding be that I am saying, "I don't eat, sleep, talk to my wife, or answer the phone in my spare time; I am continuously writing and working in my dark room."

The normal use of the present tense does not denote continuous, uninterrupted action. Certainly it can, but it does not have to. If you were to ask me where I lived, I might say, "I live in Atlanta." In that case the present tense *live* would imply a continuous action. But even then, if you saw me somewhere other than Atlanta, you would not accuse me of lying. Why? Because my use of the present tense did not mean that I continuously live every minute of my life in Atlanta. And you would not take it to mean that. Why? Because that is not the way the present tense is used in real life.

"Everyone Who Drinks . . ."

You and I are not the only ones who use the present tense in a variety of ways. Jesus did, too. In His encounter

with the woman at the well, He makes an interesting statement using the present tense. In His effort to show the
woman the superiority of living water over the water
found in Jacob's well, He says,

Everyone who *drinks* of this water shall thirst again.
—*John 4:13, emphasis mine*

The term *drinks* is present tense, which confronts us with
a curious situation. If the present tense always communicates continuous, uninterrupted action, Jesus is saying
that *those who are continuously drinking from Jacob's
well will thirst again!* That doesn't make any sense. First of
all, no one who is continually drinking gets thirsty. Second, it would be physically impossible for someone to
drink continuously from Jacob's well—or any well for that
matter.

Jesus' meaning is clear. He is referring to the normal
practice of drinking until one's thirst is quenched, then
after a period of time returning to drink again. His point is
that the water from Jacob's well would quench one's thirst
temporarily.

As you can see, it would be absurd, even contradictory,
to understand the present tense to mean continuous, uninterrupted action. That is simply not a normal rendering
of the verb tense. Certainly it can mean that, but in most
cases it does not.

Therefore, to interpret John's use of the present tense
to mean continuous, uninterrupted believing is to make
more out of the present tense than he intended. When a
man or woman believes, he or she is given eternal life—
right then and there. It is a gift. At that moment in time the
transaction is completed. As mentioned in the previous
chapter, if one must continue to believe in order to retain
possession of the gift, it is not a gift.

Think About It

*If my faith maintains
my salvation, I must ask myself,
"What must I do to maintain
my faith?" For to neglect
the cultivation of my faith
is to run the risk
of weakening or losing
my faith and thus my salvation.
I have discovered that my faith
is maintained and strengthened
by activities such as the following:
Prayer, Bible Study, Christian
Fellowship, Church Attendance,
and Evangelism.
If these and similar activities
are necessary to maintain
my faith—and the maintenance
of my faith is necessary
for salvation—how can I
avoid the conclusion
that I am saved
by my good works?*

"Believe in the Lord Jesus . . ."

There is another problem with the present tense argument. Not every reference to saving faith is in the present tense. When the Samaritan woman brought the people of the city out to hear Jesus, the text states,

> And from that city many of the Samaritans *believed* in Him . . . and many more *believed* because of His word.
> —*John 4:39–41, emphasis mine*

Here *believe* is used in the aorist tense. Unlike the present tense, the aorist tense is more indefinite. Its focus is not so much on the *time* of an event or the *continuation* of an event as it is the *fact* of the event.

When the Philippian jailer asked Paul and Silas what he must do to be saved, they did not tell him to begin believing and maintain a believing attitude. They said,

> Believe in the Lord Jesus, and you shall be saved.
> —*Acts 16:31*

Once again *believe* is in the aorist tense. The focus here is the *act* of his believing, not the maintenance of his faith or even his intention to maintain his faith. If one must keep believing to stay saved, why didn't Paul and Silas explain this fact to the jailer? Better yet, why didn't they just use the present tense to communicate the need for constant belief?

The most obvious answer is that Paul and Silas did not believe salvation was the result of continuing faith. Faith, in their thinking, was simply the door through which those desiring salvation must walk. Dr. Ryrie sums it up well:

> The New Testament always says that salvation is through faith, not because of faith (Ephesians 2:8). Faith is the channel through which we receive God's gift of forgiveness and eternal life.[1]

The Wind-blown Believer

If all this is true, what is James talking about when he says the doubter will receive nothing from God? Reread the verses in question:

> But let him ask in faith without any doubting, for the one who doubts is like the surf of the sea driven and tossed by the wind. For let not that man expect that he will receive anything from the Lord, being a double-minded man, unstable in all his ways.
> —*James 1:6–8*

A quick glance at the context of these verses clears up the confusion entirely. James is addressing Christians. And not just any Christians. These are Jewish converts undergoing trials because of their faith in Christ (see James 1:1–4).

They were responding to their trials much like we do. They were wondering why God was allowing those things to take place. James writes to encourage them to endure, to hang in there (see James 1:4). Knowing how confused they were, he asserts,

> But if any of you lacks wisdom, let him ask of God, who gives to all men generously and without reproach, and it will be given to him. —*James 1:5*

His point is, "If you are wondering what's going on, ask God. He can't wait to answer your prayer."

Then he warns them in the next three verses (vv. 6–8) not to allow their faith to waver in the midst of their trials. These verses have caused some confusion.

But notice whom these verses are referring to: "Let not *that man* expect that he will receive anything from the Lord" (emphasis mine). Who is *that man?* It is the Christian, undergoing trials, who asks the Lord for wisdom to know how to deal with the hard times. But in asking for wisdom, *that man* begins to doubt. Doubt what? Doubt all the things each of us is tempted to doubt when life starts caving in around us. Is there a God? Has He forgotten about me? Does He know what I am going through? What have I done to deserve this?

All of us are tempted to doubt when we face trials. James is saying that when we ask for wisdom in the midst of trials, we are to ask confidently. We are to approach God assuming that He is still in control and knows exactly what is going on. If we begin doubting, God will not grant us the wisdom we are asking for. Why? Because either we would not recognize it or we would not apply it. Such is the case with all double-minded men (see James 1:8).

This passage has nothing to do with salvation. In fact, the reader's salvation is assumed. Although these verses have great application for the believer, they say nothing about the nature of saving faith.

Tossed Back and Forth

All of us have periods of doubt. That is to be expected because Satan and his gang are constantly at work trying to destroy our faith. Just as he has an occasional victory in other areas of our lives, so he is likely to have an occasional victory in this area as well.[2] Zane Hodges speaks to this point:

> The New Testament is altogether clear that maintaining our faith in God involves a struggle whose outcome is not guaranteed simply by the fact that we are saved. Instead, fighting the good fight of faith is what the spiritual conflict is really all about. To think otherwise is to invite defeat on the spiritual battlefield.[3]

We are in a war. It's a war we will ultimately win, but it's a war in which there are real casualties. How comforting it is to know that though the enemy may temporarily steal our victory, he cannot touch our salvation. Having done nothing to earn it, we can do nothing to lose it!

Notes

1. Charles C. Ryrie, *So Great Salvation* (Wheaton, Ill.: Victor Books, 1989), p. 122.
2. In his book *Absolutely Free* (Grand Rapids, Mich.: Zondervan, 1989), Zane Hodges devotes an entire chapter to the concept of shipwrecked faith. He argues convincingly that Satan can completely shipwreck a believer's faith but that this in no way affects the believer's security. See chapter 9, p. 103.
3. Hodges, *Absolutely Free*, p. 104.

Do You Know?

1. *Can you give some examples to support the author's argument that it would be absurd, even contradictory, to understand the normal use of the present tense to mean continuous, uninterrupted action?*
2. *What is the* aorist *tense? How would you distinguish the* aorist *tense from the* present *tense? Give a couple of examples of the aorist tense from Scripture.*
3. *What did James mean when he said the doubter will receive nothing from God?*
4. *Does everyone have periods of doubt? Why or why not?*

10

Faithful to the Faithless

Thus far our approach to the question of whether or not a believer's faith must be enduring has been rather negative. For the most part, we have taken a defensive posture, putting forth objections to the arguments of those who hold that one's faith must be maintained to ensure the possession of eternal life.

Having dealt with the major arguments used to support the necessity of enduring faith, we have yet one more question to tackle: *Does the Scripture actually teach that regardless of the consistency of our faith, our salvation is secure?* Yes, it does, through both proposition and illustration.

"If We Are Faithless . . ."

The clearest statement on this subject is issued in Paul's second letter to Timothy:

> If we died with Him, we shall also live with Him;
> If we endure, we shall also reign with Him;
> If we deny Him, He also will deny us;
> If we are *faithless,* He remains *faithful;*
>   for He cannot deny Himself.
> *—2 Timothy 2:11–13, emphasis mine*

More than likely these four couplets were part of an early Christian hymn. Paul included them in his letter to Timothy much the same way modern authors include verses of hymns and portions of poems in their works today. Paul believed the sayings were theologically sound and would be a memorable illustration of four great truths to Timothy.

The first of the four is probably a reference to Romans 6 and Paul's teaching about our cocrucifixion with Christ. The second concerns the special reward for those who remain faithful through persecution.

The third couplet echoes Jesus' words in Matthew (see Matt. 10:33). Some have taken this as a reference to the possibility of apostasy.[1] The context, however, suggests that it is a repetition of the previous couplet, only in a negative form. In other words, just as the faithful will receive the Father's recognition and approval, so the unfaithful will lose His special recognition and approval. Thus, the reader is set up for the fourth and final couplet.

". . . He Remains Faithful"

The unfaithful believer will not receive a special place in the kingdom of Christ like those who are fortunate enough to be allowed to reign with Him. But the unfaithful believer will not lose his salvation.

The term translated "faithless" simply means "unbelieving." Interestingly enough, this verb is in the, you guessed it, present tense. And it's from the same root word used in John where believing is discussed in connection with gaining eternal life.

The apostle's meaning is evident. Even if a believer for all practical purposes becomes an unbeliever, his salvation is not in jeopardy. Christ will remain faithful.

Whoever wrote this hymn must have known this concept is difficult to accept: the holy Son of God allowing a man to retain his salvation once he has lost his faith? That is not an easy pill to swallow. To his (or her) credit, the writer of this hymn included the reason Christ will not take back His gift of eternal life: "For He cannot deny

93

Himself." The writer is alluding to the union each believer shares in the body of Christ. Once a person places trust in Christ's death as the payment for sin, he or she immediately becomes part of the body of Christ:

> For by one Spirit we were all baptized into one body, whether Jews or Greeks, whether slaves or free.—*1 Corinthians 12:13*

Christ will not deny an unbelieving Christian his or her salvation because to do so would be to deny Himself. Why? Faithful or not, every person who has at any time had saving faith is a permanent part of the body of Christ. Whatever action Christ takes against a believer, He takes against Himself, for each believer is a part of His body.

This one passage highlights four basic doctrines. First, all believers have the potential to experience the abundant life. Second, faithful believers will be rewarded for their faithfulness (see 2 Tim. 2:12). Third, unfaithful believers will be denied the recognition that would have been theirs if they had remained faithful. And last, believers who lose or abandon their faith will retain their salvation, for God remains faithful. As one source explained,

> True children of God cannot become something other than children, even when disobedient and weak. Christ's faithfulness to Christians is not contingent on their faithfulness to Him.[2]

The Perfect Illustrations

The Bible not only *states* that our salvation is secure despite our faithlessness but *illustrates* this truth as well. The weakness of these illustrations, however, is that they argue from silence. In these instances, the Bible never actually says, "Even though he lost his faith, he did not lose his salvation." But neither does the text assert that a particular person or group abandoned the faith and thus lost salvation. Thus, readers are left to decide for themselves.

Think About It

If our salvation hinges
on the consistency of our faith,
by what standard are we
to judge our consistency?

Can we have any doubts at all?
How long can we doubt?
To what degree can we doubt?
Is there a divine quota
we dare not exceed?

The strength of this argument lies in the fact that there are several individuals in the Scripture who stopped believing for a time and yet their salvation is never questioned. Even during the period of time in which their faith wavered, their eternal security is never debated.

If salvation is contingent on the continuity of faith, these narratives would have been the perfect places to set forth this significant bit of theology. Yet, as we will see, these portions of Scripture are used to confirm the very opposite view. In each case we find that God remains faithful, even to the faithless.

The Man with Failing Faith

The apostle Peter provides an excellent illustration of the verses we examined from 2 Timothy. We know that Peter was a believer. When Christ asked Peter who he thought He was, Peter answered,

> Thou art the Christ, the Son of the living God.
> —*Matthew 16:16*

And Jesus responded,

> Blessed are you, Simon Barjona, because flesh and blood did not reveal this to you, but My Father who is in heaven. And I also say to you that you are Peter, and upon this rock I will build My church. —*Matthew 16:17–18*

Peter had the correct answer to Jesus' question, and Jesus responded by promising to include him in the founding of the church.

On another occasion Jesus asked the Twelve if they would abandon Him as many of His other followers had begun to do (see John 6:67). Once again Peter's answer reveals his faith in the Savior:

> Lord, to whom shall we go? You have words of eternal life. And
> we have believed and have come to know that You are the Holy
> One of God.   —*John 6:68–69*

Peter was a believer all right, but his faith was not un-
shakable. And Jesus knew it. On the night of His arrest,
Jesus broke the news to Peter,

> Simon, Simon, behold, Satan has demanded permission to sift
> you like wheat.   —*Luke 22:31*

Then Jesus said,

> But I have prayed for you, that your *faith* may not fail; and you,
> when once you have turned again, strengthen your brothers.
>   —*Luke 22:32, emphasis mine*

Satan's attack would center on Peter's faith. Jesus anticipated that. And He anticipated Peter's temporary defeat
as well.[3] But nowhere did Peter's salvation come into
question.

Think about it. Jesus acknowledged that Peter was going to turn away from Him; that he would deny Him publicly at the most crucial time in His earthly life; and that
his faith would be dealt a severe blow. Yet His final words
to Peter were words of comfort. Peter was about to enter a
time in which his faith would be in jeopardy—but not his
salvation. Even though Peter would be faithless, Christ remained faithful!

The Doubting Prophet

In *Absolutely Free,* Zane Hodges points out another example of a believer who lost faith in Christ—John the Baptist.[4] There can be no doubt of John's faith in the Savior,
for John said,

> Behold, the Lamb of God who takes away the sin of the world!
> This is He on behalf of whom I said, "After me comes a Man who

97

has a higher rank than I, for He existed before me." . . . I have
beheld the Spirit descending as a dove out of heaven, and He
remained upon Him. . . . And I have seen, and have borne witness that this is the Son of God.   *—John 1:29–34*

The fact that John was physically born before Jesus makes
this statement significant. John acknowledged Christ as
the Savior and as God! What else could he mean when he
said, "For He existed before me"?

John the Baptist not only believed in Christ but gave
himself totally to the mission of preparing the people of
Israel for His arrival (see John 1:19–26). He was so consumed with his mission that he encouraged his own disciples to follow Christ instead (see John 1:35–38). And yet
this man, who by Christ's own admission was the greatest
man ever born among women (see Luke 7:28), began to
have second thoughts; he began to doubt. All of a sudden
he was not sure Christ was who he thought he was:

And this report concerning Him [Christ] went out all over Judea,
and in all the surrounding district. And the disciples of John re-
ported to him about all these things. And summoning two of his
disciples, John sent them to the Lord, saying, "Are you the Expected One, or do we look for someone else?" And when the
men had come to Him, they said, "John the Baptist has sent us to
You, saying, 'Are you the Expected One, or do we look for someone else?' "   *—Luke 7:17–20*

About these surprising verses, Hodges writes,

It is hard to believe one's eyes when this passage is first encoun-
tered. Here is the great prophet and forerunner of God's Christ
calling into question the very person to whom he had once given
bold testimony. . . . Clearly then, this great servant of God is
asking a question he presumably had settled decisively long ago.
His inquiry is manifestly an expression of doubt about the very
truth by which men and women are saved.[5]

John did not possess saving faith at that time in his life.
He was no longer sure that Christ was the Savior of the

world. He was having second thoughts about Christ's being the Lamb of God. But even with John's faith at an all-time low, Christ was still able to say about him,

> This [John] is the one about whom it is written, "Behold, I send My messenger before Your face, Who will prepare Your way before You." I say to you, among those born of women, there is no one greater than John. —*Luke 7:27–28*

Although Jesus said those things about John at the precise time when his faith was at its lowest ebb, Jesus never even hinted at the idea that John's salvation was in jeopardy. Instead, He praised him; He honored him with the title of prophet—and not just any prophet, but one whose coming was declared in the Old Testament.

A Firm Faith

We have heard it a thousand times:

> Your adversary, the devil, prowls about like a roaring lion, seeking someone to devour. —*1 Peter 5:8*

But have you ever wondered what the enemy is seeking to devour? The next verse tells us:

> But resist him, *firm in your faith.*—*1 Peter 5:9, emphasis mine*

Satan wants to destroy your faith. Once that is weakened or gone altogether, you are powerless against him. Your confidence is gone, and for all practical purposes you are useless to the kingdom of God.

Your faith is constantly under attack. Some battles you will win; some you will lose. At times you will feel as if you could move mountains. At other times you will find yourself crying out to God for a sign. But regardless of the shape your faith is in, your salvation is always intact. For whereas your faith is often tuned into your changing cir-

cumstances, your salvation is anchored in the unchanging
nature and grace of God.

Notes

1. For an explanation of this view, see *The Bible Knowledge Commentary* (Wheaton, Ill.: Victor Books, 1983), pp. 43, 754.
2. *The Bible Knowledge Commentary,* p. 754.
3. Jesus prayed that Peter's faith would not *fail,* which does not eliminate the possibility of Peter's faith faltering temporarily. The events that followed later that same evening indicate that Peter's faith did in fact suffer. The term translated "fail" in verse 32 is used in Luke 16:9 as well. There it describes what ultimately happens to the temporal things of this earth—they *fail.* In both cases *fail* carries with it a ring of finality. Jesus prays that Peter's faith will not fail for good. He indicates that His prayer will be answered when He says, "When once you have turned again, strengthen your brothers."
4. Zane Hodges, *Absolutely Free,* p. 105.
5. Hodges, *Absolutely Free,* p. 105.

Do You Know?

1. *Does the Scripture actually teach that regardless of the consistency of our faith, our salvation is secure? Explain.*
2. *Was the apostle Paul referring to apostasy when he wrote, "If we deny Him, He also will deny us"? Explain.*
3. *Why is it that every action Christ takes against a believer, He takes against Himself?*
4. *When did John the Baptist have doubts about Christ? How did Christ respond?*
5. *What is the state of your salvation if your faith is destroyed?*

11

The Case of the Disobedient Believer

"You mean to tell me that people can trust Christ as their Savior and then turn around and live any way they please and still go to heaven?"

In almost every discussion I have had concerning eternal security, this question has been asked in some form or another. For many, this is the real issue. The very idea that a person can trust Christ in order to get "fire insurance," with no intention of changing behavior, makes the doctrine of eternal security repugnant to them.

Such thinking is viewed by some as an attack on the holiness of God. "A holy God demands holy living from His children," they argue. "A man or woman whose lifestyle in no way demonstrates a desire for Christlikeness could not possibly have the Holy Spirit within, regardless of what was prayed or confessed in the past."

Those who hold this view perceive the doctrine of eternal security to be a license for sin. For this reason they consider eternal security a dangerous doctrine. And to be honest, the behavior of many "Christians" provides them with ample evidence to make such a claim.

Getting By

Along these same lines, some argue that the doctrine of eternal security allows people to "get by" with their sin. They get both the benefit of heaven and the pleasure of

101

sin. Eternal security is seen as a loophole in God's economy.

This line of reasoning is not only used to cast doubt on the salvation of others. It is not unusual for an individual to turn it upon himself as well. "Pastor," someone says, "I don't believe I'm saved anymore." When asked why, the person usually makes a confession of some kind. Behind the distress is the belief that God will put up with only so much from a person. After that, he is out!

Both those who reject eternal security on the basis of where it may lead others and those whose personal sin has caused them to doubt its validity are suffering from the same two theological errors. Both groups have a distorted view of God's holiness. Second, they have overlooked what the Bible teaches about rewards and heaven.

How Holy Is Holy?

Throughout this book, we have demonstrated, through Scripture and logic, why nothing in the nature of God forces Him to take back the gift of eternal life when a Christian sins. We who hold to the doctrine of eternal security are often accused of having a deficient grasp of God's holiness. In actuality, however, the opposite is true.

The doctrine of eternal security is supported by the belief that God is so infinitely holy and good that there is nothing—not one thing—we can *do* to *attain or maintain* our salvation. Salvation in every facet is by grace. It is a gift from start to finish. God's holiness is so far out of our league that even the best of our good deeds carries no weight in matters of salvation. The prophet proclaimed,

For all of us have become like one who is unclean,
And all our righteous deeds are like a filthy garment.
—Isaiah 64:6

People who want to do away with eternal security based on the argument that a sinning Christian is so offensive to

102

the holiness of God that he cannot be tolerated both elevate the works of man and depreciate the holiness of God. How? By introducing into the salvation model the necessity of good works to maintain one's salvation.

The Nature of God

When the Bible speaks of God's being holy, it refers to His nature. God, by nature, is morally perfect. Therefore, He is by nature set apart from those things that are less than perfect. *Holiness,* then, is a word of comparison. Whenever we speak of something as being perfect or separate, we always mean in relationship or comparison to something else.

Once good works are introduced in any fashion as a part of the salvation process, we are assuming a similarity in the moral goodness of man and God. In doing so, God becomes less separate or holy than in the salvation model where man's works had nothing to do with salvation. To introduce man's holiness is to deemphasize the holiness of God. To speak of man's moral efforts in conjunction with God's moral perfection is to lessen the contrast and thus downgrade God's holiness.

The doctrine of eternal security does not detract from or reduce the holiness of God. On the contrary, eternal security allows God's holiness to stand in its purest form, free from the feeble attempts of man to merit divine acceptance.

Out of the Danger Zone

"But," one may ask, "if He is so morally pure and so separate by nature from the imperfections of man, how can He tolerate sin in the lives of His followers?" The answer is found in the truth we have been emphasizing: God took care of the sin problem once and for all by punishing His Son on our behalf.

Think About It

If God's holiness compels Him to take back the gift of eternal life from certain believers because of their sin, one of two things is true: Either God compromises His holiness for a time— through their small sins— or man's good works can meet God's requirements for holiness —at least for a short period of time. In that case, Christ died needlessly.

It is true that sin results in separation, that God's holiness compels Him to disassociate Himself from the sinner. But equally true is the fact that God placed the sin of mankind on His Son and then turned His back on *Him*. Consequently, we who have accepted God's free gift no longer run the risk of being put out of the family. Christ was put out of it on our behalf. In Christ, the requirements of God's holiness have been completely fulfilled!

What's Next?

Several questions remain. If our salvation is secure, what reason is there to remain faithful? What do we say to persons who sincerely believe Christ died for them but have no use for holy living? Do Christians, in fact, get by with their sin? In the next three chapters we will examine these questions in detail.

Do You Know?

1. *Why do some people consider eternal security a "dangerous doctrine"?*
2. *What belief about God supports the doctrine of eternal security?*
3. *Why does the author say that persons who want to do away with the concept of eternal security "elevate the works of man" and "depreciate the holiness of God"?*
4. *What are we doing to God's holiness when we speak of human moral efforts in conjunction with God's moral perfection?*

12

What Do We Have to Lose?

Anyone who thinks that a believer's sins carry no eternal consequences has overlooked a major area of biblical theology. Yet I frequently encounter believers who think just that. Somewhere along the way they were taught or just assumed that heaven will be the same for everybody. As long as they are *in,* that is the only thing that matters. Eternal security becomes nothing more than a safety net, an emergency precaution. This attitude leads to the abuses of eternal security that have driven many away from the idea altogether. And understandably so.

If heaven is going to be the same for everyone, I can understand their point. We can have the best of both worlds. Granted, Christ's sacrifice ought to motivate us to follow Him in obedience. But if there are no long-term consequences for not following Him, why not partake from time to time of the pleasures of sin? What do we have to lose?

Real Christians Don't Sin

Many persons who hold to eternal security respond to this dilemma by doubting the genuineness of the person's salvation who would even consider such a response to God's grace.[1] In other words, a *real* Christian will obey Christ. Anyone who would use God's grace as an excuse to sin is not really a Christian at all.

I have heard countless sermons in which some well

meaning pastor or evangelist assured his audience that if they were participating in certain sins their salvation was not genuine. If you have heard such preaching you know what generally happens. At the end of the service the altar rail is filled—not with unbelievers, however, but with Christians whose assurance has been stripped away.

This view is simplistic, however, and skirts the real issue. If taking negative advantage of God's grace was proof that a person was not really a believer, we would all be in trouble! For example, each time we break the speed limit, we take unfair advantage of God's grace (see Rom. 13:1).

Furthermore, the New Testament is full of exhortations against sin. In every case these are addressed to believers. If *real* Christians don't or can't abuse God's grace by getting involved with sin, why warn them against it? Obviously the New Testament writers realized that Christians are as capable of sinning as the most lost of lost men.

A Question of Motivation

So, then, have we found a theological loophole? Apart from appreciation for all God has done, is there any reason to be good? Do we have anything to lose by sinning? Is there anything to gain by staying pure?

The answers to these questions become evident when a person understands the Bible's teachings on man's ultimate destiny. In most cases, individuals who are genuinely disturbed by these questions have been misinformed about two things: (1) where Christians will spend eternity, and (2) what it will be like.

Our Final Home

Most Christians believe their ultimate destiny is heaven. That is not true. Man's ultimate destiny is planet earth. When God created the heavens and the earth, He intentionally placed man on the earth. He could have put him in heaven. But God placed man here for a specific purpose: to rule over creation (see Gen. 1:28–31). The earth became man's responsibility. To make his job easier, God designed a body for man that is tailor-made for living and working on planet earth.

That was God's plan in the beginning, and nowhere in Scripture are we informed that His original plan has been altered. On the contrary, all of Scripture teaches that we are moving toward a time in which God's original plan will be fulfilled.

Our Temporary Home

When sin entered the world, death was close behind (see Rom. 5:12). Death was not a part of God's original plan for mankind. And eventually it will be done away with completely (see 1 Cor. 15:26). In the meantime, however, death is a present reality.

When a believer dies, he or she goes immediately to be with the Lord (see 2 Cor. 5:6–8). Since we know from numerous passages that Christ is seated at the right hand of God in heaven, it is safe to say that Christians go to heaven when they die (see Col. 3:1). Paul confirms this idea in his first letter to the Christians in Thessalonica:

> For if we believe that Jesus died and rose again, even so God will bring with Him those who have fallen asleep in Jesus. For this we say to you by the word of the Lord, that we who are alive, and remain until the coming of the Lord, shall not precede those who have fallen asleep. . . . Then we who are alive and remain shall be caught up together with them in the clouds to meet the Lord in the air, and thus we shall always be with the Lord.
> —*1 Thessalonians 4:14–17*

When Jesus returns for the Christians who are still alive on the earth, Paul says He will bring with Him those Christians who died earlier. This comment can mean only one thing. When Christians die, they go to heaven immediately.

108

Think About It

*If God puts a condition
on His faithfulness to us,
do we not also have a right
to put a condition on ours?
Can God really expect
more of us than He does
of Himself?*

But Christians do not stay in heaven forever. When Christ returns, He will establish a kingdom on this earth, a kingdom that will last for one thousand years (see Rev. 20:4). If, as Paul said, "we shall always be with the Lord" when He returns, it makes sense that we will be included in this kingdom. Keep in mind, this is an *earthly* kingdom (see Rev. 20:7–8). So once again, believers will make their home on earth.

When the thousand years are completed, and Satan has been defeated once and for all, God will re-create the earth:

> And I saw a new heaven and a new earth; for the first heaven and the first earth passed away, and there is no longer any sea. And I saw the holy city, new Jerusalem, coming down out of heaven from God, made ready as a bride adorned for her husband. And I heard a loud voice from the throne, saying, "Behold, the tabernacle of God is among men, and He shall dwell among them, and they shall be His people, and God Himself shall be among them."
> *—Revelation 21:1–3*

God will not only re-create the earth, He is planning to move in! Instead of men dying and going to heaven, John presents us with a picture of God packing up and coming to earth. The point is, after Christ returns, man is back on earth *forever.* Sin and death will be destroyed, thus erasing any potential division between man and his Creator. All in all, God's original plan will be fulfilled.

Think Again

What does all of this have to do with eternal security? A great deal. First of all, it answers the question *where* believers will be eternally secure. Second, it throws a theological wrench into the notion that as long as we get to heaven, that is all that matters. That is not all that matters because heaven is just a stopover. Heaven is temporary. We are all coming back one way or another.

Eternity is not a huge white room where we will all wander around looking for interesting historical figures to chat with. It is not going to be one long church service. Neither will it be one continual game of golf or softball or whatever else you enjoy doing. We will not be wearing white robes and walking around on clouds. It is not many of the things we have imagined, for we who are believers will spend eternity on earth.

So the question remains, what will it be like when God establishes His rule on earth? What *will* we do? And most important, will what we do *then* have anything to do with what we are doing *now?*

Notes

1. Some who hold to what is commonly referred to as a *Lordship salvation* position would fall into this category.

Do You Know?

1. *What do people who hold to a Lordship salvation position believe about the status of Christians who sin?*
2. *What does the author mean when he says that every time we break the speed limit we take unfair advantage of God's grace?*
3. *Is heaven or earth the ultimate destiny of Christians? Explain.*
4. *When Christians die, where do they go?*
5. *What's wrong with the notion that as long as we get to heaven that is all that matters?*

13

Every Second Counts

An old legend tells of a merchant in Bagdad who one day sent his servant to the market. Before very long the servant came back, white and trembling, and in great agitation said to his master, "Down in the market place I was jostled by a woman in the crowd, and when I turned around I saw that it was Death that jostled me. She looked at me and made a threatening gesture. Master, please lend me your horse, for I must hasten away to avoid her. I will ride to Samarra and there I will hide, and Death will not find me."

The merchant lent him his horse, and the servant galloped away in great haste. Later the merchant went down to the market place and saw Death standing in the crowd. He went over to her and asked, "Why did you frighten my servant this morning? Why did you make a threatening gesture?"

"That was not a threatening gesture," Death said. "It was only a start of surprise. I was astonished to see him in Bagdad, for I have an appointment with him tonight in Samarra."[1]

Choices

Death is life's only certainty. Even as Christians, we cannot escape its touch. But though we are not free to choose the moment of death, we have been given the opportunity to choose our destination once our appointed time arrives. The Bible presents only two options—heaven or hell. There is no third alternative.

Unknown to many Christians, however, is the fact that each of us has the opportunity to make another choice as well. In addition to choosing *where* we will spend eternity, we choose what it will be like for us once we get there.

In the preceding chapter we said there are two primary areas of theological confusion leading people to believe that the doctrine of eternal security allows Christians to get by with their sin. The first area has to do with *where* believers spend eternity. We covered that. The second area, and the focus of this chapter, is what eternity will be like for believers.

To Each His Own

Contrary to what you might have thought or been taught, eternity will not be the same for every unbeliever.[2] Neither will it be the same for every believer. In the book of Revelation, John describes one of the most awesome scenes that will ever take place in human history—the Final Judgment. Commonly referred to as the Great White Throne Judgment, this event occurs just before God destroys the earth as we know it and creates the new heaven and new earth. John writes,

> And I saw the dead, the great and the small, standing before the throne, and books were opened; and another book was opened, which is the book of life.   —*Revelation 20:12*

Notice that there were two sets of books—the "books" and the "book of life"—at the Judgment. John continues,

> And the dead were judged from the things which were written in the books, according to their deeds. And the sea gave up the dead which were in it, and death and Hades gave up the dead which were in them; and they were judged, every one of them according to their deeds.   —*Revelation 20:12-13*

113

The "books" contained all the deeds of those standing in line waiting to be judged. Each person was judged according to what he or she had and had not done. John adds,

> And if anyone's name was not found written in the book of life, he was thrown into the lake of fire. —*Revelation 20:15*

John makes an important distinction at this point. What was written in the "books" did not determine *where* a person spent eternity. That decision hinged on whether or not an individual's name appeared in the "book of life."

Two different kinds of judgment were taking place. One determined whether or not an individual was cast into the lake of fire. What the other judgment determined is not clear from this passage. What is clear, however, is that the determining factor was what a person had done in life. Everyone was judged according to his or her works.

The Book of Remembrance

That brings us to a sobering thought: Somebody is watching and taking notes! Clearly, our deeds count for something. Otherwise, why would God bother to write them down?

The prophet Malachi took comfort in the fact that God was watching. He lived in a time when the wicked were prospering and the righteous were suffering. Malachi was beginning to think that his righteous life was in vain. But God showed him differently:

> Then those who feared the LORD spoke to one another, and the LORD gave attention and heard it, and a *book of remembrance* was written before Him for those who fear the LORD and who esteem His name. . . . So you will again distinguish between the righteous and the wicked, between one who serves God and one who does not serve Him.—*Malachi 3:16, 18, emphasis mine*

Think About It

*How would you feel if you
received the same eternal
reward as a Christian
who left everything
to serve God in a foreign field
and who eventually gave his life
to reach a people
group for Christ?*

God compiled a record of those Jews who were remaining faithful and those who were falling away. But why? What difference would it make in the long run?

A Day in Court

The apostle Paul paid close attention to his conduct. He bent over backward to remain beyond reproach in the sight of both man and God. Why? Because he was so grateful for what Christ had done for him? Certainly that was part of the reason. But that was not his total motivation. He, too, believed that God was taking notes and that those notes would count for eternity. He writes,

> Therefore also we have as our ambition, whether at home or absent, to be pleasing to Him [Christ].   —*2 Corinthians 5:9*

That is a noble ambition. But what motivated it?

> For [because] we must all appear before the judgment seat of Christ, that each one may be recompensed for his deeds in the body, according to what he has done, whether good or bad.
> —*2 Corinthians 5:10*

Paul speaks here of a different judgment from the one John describes in Revelation 20. But once again each participant is called on to give account of his or her life.

Paul fills in some details that clarify the purpose of all this divine record keeping. First, when he says "we," that means believers. Second, he specifically states that this judgment is based on the "deeds in the body," that is, what was done on earth. Third, this judgment takes into consideration both the "good" and the "bad." This third point comes as a shock to many Christians who ask, "If we are forgiven, how can God take into consideration our bad deeds?"

A careful distinction must be made, and Zane Hodges explains it this way:

It is sometimes argued that the believer's sins cannot come under consideration at Christ's Judgment Seat since they are all forgiven. But this confuses the two kinds of judgment. The Christian's eternal destiny is not at issue in the judgment of believers, hence "sin" as a barrier to his entrance into eternal fellowship with God is not at issue either. But it must be kept in mind that to review and assess a life, the Judge must consider the life in its entirety. And that obviously includes the bad with the good.[3]

And last, Paul says we will all be "recompensed" for these deeds.

Recompensed

Paul uses the term translated "recompensed" in two other instances. In both, it refers to a slave's response to his master:

> With good will render service, as to the Lord, and not to men, knowing that whatever good thing each one does, this he will *receive back* from the Lord, whether slave or free.
> —*Ephesians 6:7–8, emphasis mine*

> For he who does wrong will *receive the consequences* of the wrong which he has done, and that without partiality.
> —*Colossians 3:25, emphasis mine*

In all three cases, this term carries with it the idea that God's actions toward the believer depend on the believer's faithfulness to Him. In Ephesians, God is described as doing good things for those who *do* good things. In Colossians, Paul promises that God will punish in some way Christians who do wrong.

Paul's use of this term in 2 Corinthians 5 seems to imply both ideas. God will respond to both the good and the bad. And in this particular passage the timing is clear. This reference is not to the normal consequences of sin in this life. Paul is referring to a future judgment, a judgment in which all we have done will be examined.

Jesus' words echo this idea:

Behold, I am coming quickly, and My reward is with Me, to
render to every man according to what he has done.
—*Revelation 22:12*

The word translated "render" also appears in Revelation
18. So Jesus is saying that "every man" will be paid back
for what he has done.

Where Justice Meets Grace

Does our behavior matter once we are assured of our
salvation? You bet it does. Are there any eternal consequences when a believer sins? Absolutely. Will eternity be
the same for those who follow Christ faithfully and those
who live for themselves? Not a chance.

Our God is a God of justice as well as grace. His offer of
grace is continually extended to even the most vile sinner.
But His justice moves Him to keep a careful record of
those who remain faithful and those who do not. His grace
moved Him to sacrifice His only Son to provide a way for
our salvation. But His justice causes Him to take special
note of those believers who are willing to sacrifice for His
Son.

Keep in mind we are not talking about heaven and hell.
That is a different issue altogether. Our works have nothing to do with *where* we spend eternity. But they have a
lot to do with what we can expect once we get there.

Notes

1. Peter Marshall, "John Doe," in *Disciples: Sermons for the Young in
Spirit,* ed. Catherine Marshall (New York: McGraw-Hill, 1963), pp. 219–
20.
2. Further evidence for the notion that hell will not be the same for all
its inhabitants comes from Jesus' warnings to the inhabitants of
Chorazin, Bethsaida, and Capernaum in Matthew 11. He finishes His
dialogue by saying, "It shall be more tolerable for the land of Sodom in
the day of judgment, than for you" (11:24). Clearly he has the people of

Sodom in mind here. The implication is that hell will be more tolerable for the people of Sodom than for the citizens of Capernaum.

3. Zane Hodges, *Grace in Eclipse: A Study on Eternal Rewards* (Dallas, Tex.: Redencion Viva, 1985), pp. 51–52.

Do You Know?

1. *Will eternity be the same for every unbeliever?*
2. *How is what is written in the "book of life" different from what is written in the "books" present at the Great White Throne Judgment?*
3. *What does the term translated* recompensed *mean as it is used by the apostle Paul?*
4. *Are there any eternal consequences when a believer sins? Explain.*

14

Gold, Silver, and Precious Stones

For no man can lay a foundation other than the one which is laid, which is Jesus Christ. Now if any man builds upon the foundation with gold, silver, precious stones, wood, hay, straw, each man's work will become evident; for the day will show it, because it is to be revealed with fire; and the fire itself will test the quality of each man's work. If any man's work which he has built upon it remains, he shall receive a reward. If any man's work is burned up, he shall suffer loss; but he himself shall be saved, yet so as through fire.

—*1 Corinthians 3:11–15*

This statement is one of the strongest supporting eternal security to be found in the entire Bible. In this passage the apostle Paul relates what will happen at the judgment seat of Christ. Every believer's life will be evaluated on the basis of his or her contribution and commitment to the kingdom of God—of which Christ is pictured as the foundation.

Two kinds of Christians are portrayed here. The first man who steps up to be evaluated represents those who have made real contributions to God's kingdom during their earthly lives. His works are described as "gold, silver, [and] precious stones." They are of such quality that they survive the intense examination of the Savior. Consequently, this man is rewarded for his faithfulness.

Then the second man steps up. He represents believers who have no time for the things of Christ, who live their lives for themselves. One by one his deeds are evaluated, and one by one they burn. His works are described as "wood, hay, [and] straw." His works have no real substance, no eternal value.

When the smoke clears, he is faced with the reality that in God's estimation, nothing he has lived for has counted. He has spent his entire life pursuing things. His earthly success has focused on those things that are perishable, temporary.

Paul says this man will suffer loss. That is, he will have nothing to show for his life; he will have lost everything. But, Paul concludes, the man himself will be saved!

This passage is so powerful because we are presented with a Christian who at no point in his entire life bore any eternal fruit. And yet his salvation is never jeopardized. There is never a question about where he will spend eternity.

Good News, Bad News

Despite his secure position as a child of God, this individual probably did not leave the scene rejoicing. His entire life was written off as a heap of smoldering kindling. And to make things even worse, his Savior, to whom he owed everything, acted as his Judge. This man truly suffered loss.

And it did not end there. For Scripture tells us that a man's faithfulness or unfaithfulness in this life results in a great deal more than simply a moment of rejoicing or shame at the judgment seat of Christ. What takes place at the judgment seat has enduring consequences.

The Reward of Authority

The Gospels are full of parables illustrating this very point. One such parable focuses on a landowner who entrusted his possessions to three slaves while he was gone on a journey (see Matt. 25:14–30). He gave each slave a

121

different amount to care for, an amount warranted by individual ability.

The first two slaves invested their master's possessions and doubled their investments. The third slave, however, buried his master's talent in the ground.

After a long time the master returned and called for the slaves to settle their accounts. Having heard the reports of the first two slaves, the master responded by saying to each one,

> Well done, good and faithful slave; you were faithful with a few things, I will put you in charge of many things; enter into the joy of your master.   *—Matthew 25:23*

The two slaves had been entrusted with different amounts. Yet they both received the same reward. From this outcome, we gain insight into God's standard for judgment. Each of us will be judged on the basis of individual opportunities and abilities (see v. 15). This fact is underscored by the master's reaction to the third slave.

With his head hanging low, the third slave approached his master:

> Master, I knew you to be a hard man, reaping where you did not sow, and gathering where you scattered no seed. And I was afraid, and went away and hid your talent in the ground; see you have what is yours.   *—Matthew 25:24–25*

He had done nothing with his master's talent. He had not even *tried* to do anything with it. His master replied,

> You wicked, lazy slave. . . . You ought to have put my money in the bank. . . . Therefore take away the talent from him, and give it to the one who has the ten talents.
>   *—Matthew 25:26–28*

At that point in the parable Jesus detoured to make a comment. He knew His listeners would wonder why the slave with ten talents was given one more. One would

Think About It

What are you doing that will count for eternity?

think the slave with four would have received it. But that is not the way things will be done in His kingdom:

> For to everyone who has shall more be given, and he shall have an abundance; but from the one who does not have, even what he does have shall be taken away.　　—*Matthew 25:29*

It was Jesus' way of illustrating what happened to the man who came to the judgment seat with wood, hay, and straw. When the judgment was over, even that was taken away.

Christ's meaning is clear: *Those who demonstrate in this life an ability and willingness to properly use and invest what God has entrusted to them will be given more to use and invest in His future kingdom.* The first two slaves were faithful with a few things. Their reward was the opportunity to be faithful with even more.

The Outer Darkness

The final verse of this parable is so severe that many commentators assume it is a description of hell. It is not. Keep in mind that this is a parable. A parable is used to make one central point. The point of this parable is that in God's future kingdom, those who were faithful in this life will be rewarded and those who were not will lose any potential reward. Some will be given more privileges and responsibility while others will have none.

Here is the verse:

> And cast out the worthless slave into the outer darkness; in that place there shall be weeping and gnashing of teeth.
> 　　—*Matthew 25:30*

Jesus concluded his parable and added that the slave was cast out into the outer darkness. Then referring to the actual place, which the "outer darkness" in the parable refers to, Jesus stated, "In that place there shall be weeping and gnashing of teeth."

Before we can understand the full impact of the parable, we must first determine what the "outer darkness" refers to in the context of the parable.[1] It certainly does not mean hell in the parable. How could a master throw a slave into hell? This phrase appears in a similar parable in chapter 22. In that parable an unwanted guest is bound and thrown out of a banquet hall into the "outer darkness" (see Matt. 22:13); it clearly refers to being thrown outside a building into the dark.

The same interpretation would fit in the case of the lazy slave. Whereas two of the slaves were given more responsibility, the third one was thrown out of the house.

But what *actual* place was Jesus referring to in the parable? He gave us only one hint: "In that place there shall be weeping and gnashing of teeth." There is no mention of punishment as in the parable following this one (see Matt. 25:46). There is no mention of pain or fire or worms. This place is clearly not hell. Well, then, where is it?

Believers in the Kingdom

Before answering this important question, I want to make sure you understand the full implication of the two passages we have just surveyed. *The kingdom of God will not be the same for all believers.* Let me put it another way. Some believers will have rewards for their earthly faithfulness; others will not. Some believers will be entrusted with certain privileges; others will not. Some will reign with Christ; others will not (see 2 Tim. 2:12). Some will be rich in the kingdom of God; others will be poor (see Luke 12:21, 33). Some will be given true riches; others will not (see Luke 16:11). Some will be given heavenly treasures of their own; others will not (see Luke 16:12). Some will reign and rule with Christ; others will not (see Rev. 3:21).

A careful study of these passages reveals one common denominator. Privilege in the kingdom of God is determined by one's faithfulness in this life. This truth may come as a shock. Maybe you have always thought that everyone would be equal in the kingdom of God. It is true that there will be equality in terms of our inclusion in the kingdom of God but not in our rank and privilege.

The clearest proof comes from Jesus' reply to Peter when he asked the Master about what he and the other apostles would receive for their sacrifices:

> Then Peter answered and said to Him, "Behold, we have left everything and followed You; what then will there be for us?"
> —*Matthew 19:27*

Jesus did not reprimand him for being selfish and self-centered. Neither did He attempt to correct Peter's theology. Peter's question was justified. So Jesus answered,

> Truly I say to you, that you who have followed Me, in the regeneration when the Son of Man will sit on His glorious throne, you also shall sit upon twelve thrones, judging the twelve tribes of Israel. —*Matthew 19:28*

The apostles will have a special position of authority in the future kingdom. You and I will not judge the twelve tribes of Israel. That is a privilege reserved for that special group.

Weeping and Gnashing of Teeth

Now, back to our original question. Where is this place represented by the "outer darkness" in Jesus' parables? To be in the "outer darkness" is *to be in the kingdom of God but outside the circle of men and women whose faithfulness on this earth earned them a special rank or position of authority.*

The "outer darkness" represents not so much an actual place as it does a sphere of influence and privilege.[2] It is not a geographical area in the kingdom where certain men and women are consigned to stay. It is simply a figure of speech describing their low rank or status in God's kingdom.

The reason there will be weeping and gnashing of teeth by those who find themselves in this position becomes obvious once we eliminate some confusion over the phrase "gnashing of teeth." This figure of speech does not symbolize pain as many have thought.

The best example of what it really denotes is found at the end of Stephen's sermon in Acts. Stephen had been falsely accused of blasphemy. After his long defense, his accusers were "cut to the quick, and they began gnashing their teeth at him" (Acts 7:54). Why? Because they were in pain? No, because "they were unable to cope with the wisdom and the Spirit with which he was speaking" (Acts 6:10). Those men heard the truth, knew they were in error, and could not take it. They were extremely frustrated with themselves. But instead of repenting, they silenced the voice of truth.

Now, imagine standing before God and seeing all you have lived for reduced to ashes. How do you think you would feel? How do you think you would respond? Picture yourself watching saint after saint rewarded for faithfulness and service to the King—and all the time knowing that you had just as many opportunities but did nothing about them.

We cannot conceive of the agony and frustration we would feel if we were to undergo such an ordeal; the realization that our unfaithfulness had cost us eternally would be devastating. And so it will be for many believers.

Just as those who are found faithful will rejoice, so those who suffer loss will weep. As some are celebrated for their faithfulness, others will gnash their teeth in frustration over their own shortsightedness and greed.

We do not know how long this time of rejoicing and sorrow will last. Those whose works are burned will not weep and gnash their teeth for eternity. At some point we know God will comfort those who have suffered loss (see Rev. 21:4). But there is no indication from Scripture that everyone will share the same privileges for eternity. The rewards are permanent.

"Do Not Be Deceived . . ."

It may seem strange that in a book on eternal security I would devote so much space to the judgment and rewards of believers. But I believe that this area of doctrine is the key to reconciling God's justice with the free gift of salvation. Anyone who takes Jesus' kingdom teaching seriously knows that believers do not get away with sin. Every sinful deed will be examined. On the other side of the coin, we can rest assured that none of our good deeds will go unnoticed, either.

Several years ago I did a series in our church on the topic of rewards. As the series progressed, I began to notice a change taking place in the life of one of our high-school students. Ken had never been much of a spiritual leader in our Youth Department. In fact, I learned later that up until that time, he had for the most part gone the way of the world. But something about the series caught his attention. Every week he moved closer and closer to the front of the sanctuary. By the end of the series, he was on the first row.

In the weeks that followed, I had several opportunities to talk to Ken. During our time together, he shared with me details of his spiritual pilgrimage and why he believed the series on rewards had such an effect on him. He said,

I was always under the assumption that as long as a person had trusted Christ, and knew he was going to heaven, that was pretty much it. I figured that in heaven we would all be equal. That being the case, I really didn't see any point in giving up anything down here. What difference would it make? When you began talking about rewards I was shocked. I had never heard anything like that before. All of a sudden I started thinking about everything I did. I began to realize that every moment counted. I quit drinking. I quit going to parties. I started inviting my friends to church. Everything changed. I guess before that, I really wasn't motivated. Once I realized that what I do now determines what eternity will be like, I got busy.

Today Ken is in college. He has made a significant impact for Christ in his fraternity as well as on his campus in general. Every time I see him I can't help wondering how many other Kens are in my congregation and in congregations all over this country. Believers who have been lulled into thinking that once they have a ticket to heaven, they can relax; who see no connection between their lives now and eternity; who face the embarrassment of seeing all they have lived for reduced to wood, hay, and straw.

Jim Elliot understood the big picture. By sacrificing his life in an attempt to evangelize the Auca Indians, he became an illustration of his own words when he said,

> He is no fool who gives what he cannot keep to gain what he cannot lose.

Every moment counts. No deed goes unnoticed. All of us must give an account. No one gets by with anything. If you are a believer living for Christ, this news should be encouraging. If, however, you are one of those believers who has been content just to know you are on your way to heaven, this information should be disturbing. It is my prayer that you will renew your commitment to Christ and begin living for Him. Heed Paul's words:

> Do not be deceived, God is not mocked; for whatever a man sows, this he will also reap. . . . And let us not lose heart in doing good, for in due time we shall reap if we do not grow weary. —*Galatians 6:7–9*

Notes

1. It is a common error when interpreting parables and illustrations to confuse the figurative details of the illustration with elements in the

real world. This tendency to bring details from the realm of the imaginary to the real world causes undue confusion. Jesus' reference to the branch that was thrown into the fire and burned in John 15 is a good example. Some have interpreted His words to mean believers who do not bear fruit are removed from the body of Christ and eventually thrown into hell. Hodges comments,

> This statement (John 15:6) has caused needless perplexity. The main reason for that is the strong impulse many readers have to identify the reference with fire to hell. . . . There is no reason at all to think of the fire as literal, just as we are not dealing with a literal vine, literal branches, or literal fruit. "Fire" here is simply another figurative element in the horticultural metaphor. *(Absolutely Free* [Grand Rapids, Mich.: Zondervan, 1989], p. 135)

The unfruitful believer is set aside, shelved. He or she is of no practical use to Christ or to His kingdom—just as an unfruitful branch is of no use to a fruit-producing vine.
2. For more on this view of "outer darkness," see Zane Hodges, *Grace in Eclipse: A Study on Eternal Rewards* (Dallas, Tex.: Redencion Viva, 1985), pp. 86–95.

Do You Know?

1. *What two types of believers are represented by "gold, silver, and precious stones" and "wood, hay, and straw"?*
2. *In the parable of the talents, why was the slave with the most money given even more? What point was Christ making?*
3. *Will the kingdom of God be the same for all believers? Explain.*
4. *According to the author, what does the* outer darkness *in Jesus' parables represent?*
5. *What does the phrase* gnashing of teeth *mean?*

15

The Unpardonable Sin

Through the years I have talked with many Christians and non-Christians who were afraid they had committed "the unpardonable sin." Just about everyone had a different understanding of exactly what that was. But they all agreed on one thing: They were guilty and felt that theirs was a hopeless situation. Christians who believe they have committed the unpardonable sin have a difficult—if not impossible—time accepting the doctrine of eternal security. For this reason I felt compelled to deal with the issue.

Hundreds of verses in the Bible promise the forgiveness of our sins, but only one passage refers to an unforgivable sin. Let's examine the passage to gain insight into what Jesus meant when He referred to a sin that cannot be forgiven.

"It Shall Not Be Forgiven"

Jesus had healed a demon-possessed man who was blind and dumb, "so that the dumb man spoke and saw" (Matt. 12:22). The multitudes following Jesus began to say, "This man cannot be the Son of David, can he?" The implication was that they believed He was the son of David, in other words, the Messiah.

On the other hand, the Pharisees accused Jesus of casting out demons by Beelzebul, the ruler of the demons. Jesus' response to their accusation led Him to conclude,

> Therefore I say to you, any sin and blasphemy shall be forgiven men, but blasphemy against the Spirit shall not be forgiven. And whoever shall speak a word against the Son of Man, it shall be forgiven him; but whosoever shall speak against the Holy Spirit, it shall not be forgiven him, either in this age, or in the age to come. —*Matthew 12:31–32*

The term *blasphemy* may be defined "defiant irreverence." We would apply the term to such sins as cursing God or willfully degrading things considered holy. In this passage the term refers to the declaration of the Pharisees who had witnessed undeniable evidence that our Lord was performing miracles in the power of the Holy Spirit. Yet they attributed the miracles to Satan. In the face of irrefutable evidence they ascribed the work of the Holy Spirit to that of Satan.

I agree with a host of biblical scholars that this unique circumstance cannot be duplicated today. The Pharisees had seen proof after proof that Christ was who He claimed to be. They couldn't escape the fact that what He was doing was supernatural in nature. But instead of acknowledging what I believe they knew in their hearts was true, they attributed the supernatural power to that of Satan instead of the Holy Spirit. That, in a sense, was the last straw.

Christ is not in the world as He was then. Although the Holy Spirit is still accomplishing supernatural things through His servants, they are merely representatives of the King. The circumstances of Matthew 12 make it impossible for this sin to take place today. This incident, I might add, is the only one in which a sin is declared unforgivable. The Bible clearly states, "For whoever will call upon the name of the Lord will be saved" (Rom. 10:13). No invitation to salvation carries with it an exception clause, "unless you have committed the unpardonable sin."

No matter how evil our sins, there is pardon for them. God forgave David for his adultery, dishonesty, and murder (see 2 Sam. 12:13; Ps. 51). He forgave the prodigal for his "loose living" (see Luke 15:11–32). Simon Peter's triple denial of our Lord accompanied by profanity was forgiven (see Matt. 26:74–75). The apostle Paul was forgiven of his preconversion merciless persecution of Christians (see Acts 9:1).

Although there is no unpardonable sin, there is an unpardonable state—the state of unbelief. There is no pardon for a person who dies in unbelief.

What About You?

If you are concerned that you have committed the unpardonable sin, you can rest assured you have not. Your concern confirms your innocence. God always welcomes those whose hearts are sensitive toward Him.

On the other hand, if you fear that you might possibly be in the unpardonable state of unbelief, that can be remedied this very moment. You have read enough by now to know that salvation is by faith alone—faith in the death of Christ as the full payment for your sin. If you are not sure you have trusted Christ as your Savior, why not turn back to the end of chapter 8 and pray the prayer we have included there?

Do You Know?

1. *How does the author define the term* blasphemy?
2. *Is it possible to commit the "unpardonable sin" today? Explain.*
3. *Why does the author say there is no "unpardonable sin," but rather an "unpardonable state"?*
4. *What assurance does the author give to those who worry that they may have committed the unpardonable sin?*

Think About It

*If there is an unpardonable sin,
Christ did not die for all sin.
If He did not die for all sin,
there are those to whom
salvation is not available.
If salvation is not available
to all men, John 3:16 and
a multitude of other
New Testament verses
are not true.*

16

Falling from Grace

You have been severed from Christ, you who are seeking to be justified by law; you have fallen from grace. —*Galatians 5:4*

Don was a new member in our church. He had not been a Christian for very long when he joined. "Dr. Stanley," he asked, "how does a person know if he has fallen from grace?"

That was not the first time I had been asked this question. I imagine every pastor who has been in the ministry for any length of time has heard it.

"What do you mean?" I asked.

"I mean, well, you know. I just don't feel it anymore. I used to be close to God, but then I got involved with some things and . . ."

"You're not sure you're still saved."

"Yeah, I guess that's it."

"Falling" Out of Context

For many people "falling from grace" is synonymous with losing salvation. This perception is unfortunate. Equally unfortunate is that the majority of people I talk to about "falling from grace" have no idea where the phrase came from or to what it originally referred. In most cases they aren't even sure where they first heard it. "Doesn't the Bible say you can fall from grace?" they ask.

To compound the problem, these three words have become a common expression for losing favor with someone. All of this together has resulted in a great deal of confusion over this phrase, which appears only once in the New Testament and was never intended to be lifted from the text as a theological maxim. To understand this highly misunderstood expression, we must look at its one and only context.

An Impossible Combination

The book of Galatians finds Paul defending himself and the gospel of Christ from a group of "teachers" who arrived in Galatia sometime after he left. The group, commonly referred to as the Judaizers, proclaimed a gospel different from Paul's. Yet it was similar to the apostle's teaching in enough ways to confuse the Christians in Galatia.

The group believed and taught that salvation was found through having faith in Christ along with keeping portions of the law. Their distorted gospel centered on the importance of circumcision. Paul's letter indicates that the Judaizers were successful in persuading some gentile believers to be circumcised to ensure their salvation (see Gal. 5:2).

The series of events broke the apostle's heart (see Gal. 4:18–20). He was under the impression that the people of Galatia were solid in their understanding of the gospel. To hear that they were so easily led astray was a real blow to Paul. He wrote,

> I am amazed that you are so quickly deserting Him who called you by the grace of Christ for a different gospel; which is really not another; only there are some who are disturbing you, and want to distort the gospel of Christ.   —*Galatians 1:6-7*

How Different?

It is impossible for us to know all the Judaizers believed. Numerous scholars have researched this question in an attempt to piece together their theology. Although they don't see eye to eye on all the details, there are a couple areas of agreement.

To begin with, the Judaizers believed in salvation by works. It was not enough to simply put one's trust in Christ's death on the cross as payment for sin. They taught that a man must combine his faith with works in order to gain eternal life.

Second, the Judaizers continued to adhere to portions of the law as a code of ethics. They observed special days. They retained many of the law's dietary guidelines. And as mentioned earlier, circumcision was significant to the Judaizers. From what Paul said in Galatians, the topic must have been one of their favorites.

A Heavy Load

So, what has all of this to do with falling from grace? Within the context of this great debate Paul makes his statement concerning falling from grace. Please take note. *Paul's primary concern was not that the Galatian believers were drifting off into some sort of gross immorality.* His fear was not that they were consciously abandoning God. That was not the point of contention. In one sense, the opposite was true. They were about to adopt a form of religion that restricted their freedom even further! They were in danger of committing themselves to a way of life that would demand more in the way of works. He warned,

> It was for freedom that Christ set us free; therefore keep standing firm and do not be subject again to a yoke of slavery.
> —*Galatians 5:1*

Interestingly enough, this verse serves as the introduction to the passage including the expression under discussion. Paul continued,

Think About It

*If falling from grace indicates
the loss of salvation,
why is there no mention of hell?
The only threat Paul makes
is a return to the "yoke of
slavery."
As bad as that might be,
the threat of hell would
certainly carry a great deal more
incentive than the possibility
of a lifetime of law keeping.
Besides, the Jews
in Paul's audience
were used to living
under the law.*

Behold I, Paul, say to you that if you receive circumcision, Christ will be of no benefit to you. And I testify again to every man who receives circumcision, that he is under obligation to keep the whole Law.   —*Galatians 5:2-3*

What did he mean when he said that *Christ will be of no benefit to those who receive circumcision?* Paul was born in a Jewish home. He was circumcised. Furthermore, Paul had Timothy circumcised to keep from giving offense to the Jews (see Acts 16:3). What was he getting at?

Circumcision had been presented to the group as a means of salvation. In effect Paul was warning them that trusting circumcision for salvation was a waste of time. That was not the way to find acceptance in Christ. Anyone who was circumcised for salvation was adding works to faith, thus demonstrating a lack of faith in the sufficiency of Christ's death. The act of circumcision was not the problem. It was the bad theology attached to the act that concerned him.

"Besides," he argued, "you can't just pick and choose which parts of the law you want to keep and which parts you want to dispose of. If you think salvation comes through the law, you'd better keep the whole thing." It was all or nothing. Combining Christ and the law wouldn't work because they were two entirely different systems. Law and grace don't mix. A gift is not a gift if you have to do something to get it.

Severed from the Savior

Then Paul used strong language:

You have been severed from Christ, you who are seeking to be justified by law; you have *fallen from grace.*
                           —*Galatian 5:4, emphasis mine*

The situation demanded forthrightness. They were choosing to go right back into the bondage from which they had

139

been freed through Christ's death. If salvation could be attained through the route offered by the Judaizers, Christ died needlessly (see Gal. 2:21).

That is exactly the point Paul makes by including the term translated "severed." It is difficult to find a good English equivalent for this term within this sentence structure. The word really means "nullify."[1] But to say, "You have been nullified from Christ," does not make sense in English. The New International Version uses the term *alienated,* but that does not quite explain it well, either.

To paraphrase the apostle's words, "Your association with Christ has been nullified."[2] To nullify something is to eliminate its value, impact, significance or, in some cases, consequence. *By integrating portions of the law into the gospel, they were nullifying the need for Christ's death for their sin.* Again, if salvation could be attained through the law, there was no reason for Christ to die.

Paul was building on what he had said in the previous verse. Once again I paraphrase, "You cannot pick and choose which portions of the law you want to obey. It is all or none! And if you choose the way of the law, you nullify the death of Christ." The King James Version is helpful here: "Christ is become of no effect unto you." In other words, "What good is Christ if you choose to be justified by law?"

At that point Paul stated, "You have fallen from grace." To clarify his meaning, let's ask a simple question: To what? If they have fallen *from* grace, to what had they fallen? Well, what has he been contrasting grace with all along? Works and law.

In this context the opposite of grace is not lost. That does not even make sense grammatically. The opposite of grace is the works of the law. To *fall from grace, then, is to abandon the salvation by grace model for justification and to adopt the salvation by works model.* The New International Version says, "You have fallen away from grace." One commentator observes,

140

The issue here is not the possible loss of salvation for grace is referred to not as salvation itself but as a method of salvation. . . . If the Galatians accepted circumcision as necessary for salvation, they would be leaving the grace system for the Mosaic Law system.[3]

Paul wasn't threatening them with the loss of salvation, just a loss of freedom (see Gal. 5:1). He didn't say they were falling from salvation. His concern was that they were falling away from God's system of grace, which in turn would lead them right back into the frustration of living under the law.

Falling from Grace Today

Not surprisingly, I have never heard the following complaint: "Pastor, I have fallen from grace. I feel like I need to be at church every time the doors are open." Nor have I heard, "Pastor, I have fallen from grace. I feel I must keep portions of the Mosaic law to be justified." Silly? Maybe, but to fall from grace in the way Paul meant, these are the types of things a person would need to experience.

Falling from grace has absolutely nothing to do with falling into sin. It has more to do with falling into error.

Inseparable

Dear Christian, you may fall from grace, but you will never fall from salvation. That is for certain. How do I know? For one thing, the same man who warned one group against falling from grace assured another group of the unalterability of their salvation:

But in all these things we overwhelmingly conquer through Him who loved us. For I am convinced that neither death, nor life, nor angels, nor principalities, nor things present, nor things to come, nor powers, nor height, nor depth, nor any other created thing, shall be able to separate us from the love of God, which is in Christ Jesus our Lord.   —*Romans 8:37–39*

141

I don't think Paul left anything out. If he did, it certainly wasn't intentional. If you have put your faith in Christ as your Savior, NOTHING can separate you from the love of Christ. And you can't get more secure than that!

Notes

1. Other passages where this term appears are Galatians 3:17; Romans 3:3, 31; 2 Corinthians 3:11, 13, 14; and Ephesians 2:15. In each case two things are brought into conflict. The result is that one *nullifies* the effect or impact of the other.
2. F. F. Bruce, *The New International Greek Testament Commentary, Commentary on Galatians* (Grand Rapids, Mich.: Eerdmans, 1982), p. 231.
3. *The Bible Knowledge Commentary,* p. 605.

Do You Know?

1. *Why did the Judaizers' gospel center on the importance of circumcision?*
2. *How would you explain the concept of* falling *from* grace?
3. *What is the opposite of* grace?
4. *Is there a connection between* falling *from grace* and *falling into sin?*

17

Hebrews: A Unique Situation

On five separate occasions the author of the book of Hebrews warns his readers of the perils of abandoning the Christian faith. Three of these passages form a major part of the scriptural arsenal used by those who believe a person can lose salvation. An in-depth study of Hebrews is certainly beyond the scope of this book. But at the same time I feel it would be unfair to address our subject without providing an explanation of these important verses.

A Word About Method

No verse of Scripture was penned without a specific purpose in mind. Luke wrote his gospel to provide his readers with a chronologically accurate account of the life of Christ (see Luke 1:3–4). John wrote his gospel so that people would believe that Jesus was the Christ (see John 20:30–31). They wrote with not only a purpose in mind but a specific audience as well. Each of Paul's epistles was carefully crafted to meet the particular needs of the specific church he was addressing. His letter to the people in Corinth would not have been suited for the church in Ephesus. Admittedly, principles in each of his letters are universally applicable. But the specifics were obviously written with one group in mind.

Identifying an author's purpose and audience is a great aid in interpretation. Sometimes an author informs us of both at the outset of a book. Other times we are left to hunt for these treasures by working through the details of the text. The author of the book of Hebrews does not come right out and tell us who his audience is and why he feels compelled to write. However, even a cursory reading of the text reveals both his intended audience and his purpose for writing.

The Audience

In all probability, the audience addressed in Hebrews was primarily Jewish Christians. This view is supported by several themes that surface throughout the book. First, the author continually insists that the old covenant was obsolete. It would be pointless to keep hammering away on this issue if the audience was primarily gentile. A gentile audience would have put no stock in a Jewish covenant to begin with. So why work so hard to convince them that it had been done away with?

Second, the author continually supports his argument with references to the Old Testament Scriptures. Anyone who has been involved in evangelism knows how ineffectual it is to use Scripture to support a premise when the person with whom you are sharing does not consider the Bible a trustworthy source of information. The author of Hebrews was clearly under the assumption that his references to the Old Testament would carry weight with his audience.

Third, the author indicates on several occasions a concern that his readers may walk away from their dependency on Christ and return to Judaism. That would not be a concern if his readers were primarily gentile. As one commentator writes,

> Converts to Christianity from paganism, on the other hand, adopted the Old Testament as their sacred book along with the Christian faith; if they were tempted to give up their Christian faith, the Old Testament would go with it.[1]

If Gentiles abandoned the faith, they would return no doubt to that form of religion from which they had originally been converted. There would be no reason to fear that they would adopt the religion of the Jews.

The Author's Purpose

The predominantly Jewish audience had evidently never seen or heard Jesus personally (see Heb. 2:3). As a result of their conversion, they faced intense opposition. They experienced insult, prison, and even the confiscation of their property (see Heb. 10:32–34). Through it all, they remained faithful to their newfound faith.

But then something happened that hindered their spiritual progress. They became disillusioned with Christianity. They began to drift away (see Heb. 2:1). Apparently, their tendency was to retreat back to Judaism where their religious practices would be protected by Rome.[2]

So the author of Hebrews sets out in his letter *to persuade his brothers and sisters to keep the faith.* He begins by pointing to Christ's superiority over the Old Testament prophets, the angels, and even Moses. He then argues for the superiority of Christ's priesthood to that of both Melchizedek and Aaron. From there he demonstrates the preeminence of the new covenant over the old. And he ends the book by encouraging his readers to remain faithful in light of those who have gone before them.

Interspersed within this tightly woven argument are five passages that serve as warnings to those who either "drift" or "fall" away from their faith in Christ. The author, in an attempt to be comprehensive, wants his readers to know the consequences of turning their backs on God's new covenant, ratified through the blood of His Son.

This book is relevant to our discussion because these warnings are *not* given to a group of people trying to make up their minds about who Christ is for the first time. At some point in the past the group expressed sincere

Think About It

*Assuming for the moment
that you have young children,
would you discipline a child
who acknowledged you
as their authority
differently from the one
who refused to acknowledge
your right to exercise authority?*

*Which, if either, would receive
the more severe punishment?*

faith in Christ. They were sincere enough to suffer. The warnings in Hebrews are directed toward men and women who have believed. In that way their struggle parallels the experience of many believers today. But there is a significant difference as well.

The question with which the group was struggling was *not* whether to abandon God and live a life of sin. The group was not being led away from Christ by the enticement of sin's pleasures. In abandoning Christianity, the people would return to a form of religion that had a great deal to say about sin and its consequences. I rarely meet Christians who abandon Christianity to get involved with a religious group that demands more from them and allows less freedom. It is usually the other way around. In this way the audience for which the book of Hebrews was written differs from most people who fall away from the faith.

The warning passages, then, were intended primarily for those who were abandoning Christianity as a way of life. The intent of the warnings was to show the consequences of abandoning faith in Christ for anything else, whether it be Judaism, sin, or some other religion.

I stress all of this because many people use the warning passages in Hebrews as proof texts for the idea that a person can lose his or her salvation by falling into sin. The author's primary concern for his readers was not the threat of their falling into some particular sin. The author of Hebrews was concerned that his audience might walk away from Christianity altogether and return to Judaism, thus his emphasis on the superiority of Christ and the new covenant.

In the following chapters we will look at what the book of Hebrews teaches about salvation. Then we will examine the three warning passages that are sometimes used to support the notion that a believer's salvation can be lost. We will carefully study each one in light of who the author was addressing and why he was addressing them.

Notes

1. F. F. Bruce, *The Epistle to the Hebrews* (Grand Rapids, Mich.: Eerdmans, 1964), p. xxvii.
2. Bruce, *Epistle to the Hebrews,* p. xxx.

Do You Know?

1. *What three reasons does the author give for concluding that Jewish Christians were the primary audience for Hebrews?*
2. *What are some of the arguments the writer of Hebrews uses to persuade his brothers and sisters to keep the faith?*
3. *How do the people to whom the book of Hebrews is addressed differ from most people who fall away from the faith?*
4. *What was the writer of Hebrews concerned would happen if he was unable to persuade the people to keep the faith?*

18

Once and For All

If the author of Hebrews did not believe in eternal security, we can only assume that he would be consistent in his view throughout his epistle. That is, he would not say one thing in one part of his letter and something else later on. A person cannot believe in eternal security and disbelieve it at the same time. However, a person can believe one way and be misinterpreted to the point of making him sound as if he believes the very opposite.

On several occasions I have picked up a newspaper to read a column on what *I* supposedly believe or said about a particular issue. Those who know me recognize immediately that I have been misquoted or that somebody misinterpreted what I said. Those who don't know me are left to weigh what they read against what they have heard from other, and hopefully more reliable, sources.

To get an accurate picture of what the writer of Hebrews believed about eternal security, we cannot limit ourselves to a few verses. We must take into account the message of the entire book. Other than the book of John, no New Testament book argues so conclusively in favor of eternal security. In several places the author states that what the blood of animals could not accomplish (i.e., forgiveness), the death of Christ achieved. Furthermore, what at one time had to be repeated over and over again was done once and for all at Calvary (see Heb. 9:26–27; 10:9–14, 18).

The Blood of Bulls and Goats

One passage in particular, Hebrews 10:1–18, seems to sum up the author's thoughts on the extent of our salvation. He compares the inadequacies of the sacrificial system with what was attained through Christ's death. He says that the continual animal sacrifices offered year after year could never "make perfect" those who participate in them (see Heb. 10:1). To "make perfect" here refers to the removal of guilt, which is a process necessary to prepare man to enter into a relationship with a perfect God. Our imperfectionsdisqualify us from a relationship with God. Yet animal sacrifice could not erase those imperfections.

Then he makes an incredible statement:

> Otherwise, would they [animal sacrifices] not have ceased to be offered, because the worshipers, having once been *cleansed,* would no longer have had *consciousness of sins?*
> —*Hebrews 10:2, emphasis mine*

In stating two of the inadequacies of animal sacrifice, the author gives us keen insight into one of the benefits of Christ's sacrifice. When a sinner is finally "cleansed" of his or her sin, he or she will no longer have any "consciousness of sins." The term *cleansed* is in a verb tense that means "cleansed once and for all."[1] A person who had been through this process would never have to be *cleansed* again. The author doesn't sound as if he believes a Christian can lose salvation. If an individual loses salvation, he or she would surely have to be *cleansed* again.

But what about the idea of no longer having any "consciousness of sins"? Does he mean that a person who experiences absolute cleansing is no longer aware of sin? No. This statement is made in contrast to the statement that follows in verse 3:

> But in those sacrifices there is a reminder of sins year by year.

His point is that animal sacrifice was an annual *reminder* of one's guilt, but what was needed was a once and for all sacrifice that removed the guilt.

Cleansed Once and For All

Having pointed out the inadequacies of animal sacrifice, the author moves on to explain the sufficiency of Christ's sacrifice. His sacrifice accomplished the very things the blood of bulls and goats could not:

> By this will we have been sanctified through the offering of the body of Jesus Christ once for all . . . but He, having offered one sacrifice for sins *for all time,* sat down at the right hand of God.
> —*Hebrews 10:10, 12, emphasis mine*

Once again the author uses a verb tense that denotes a one-time action with continuing results: "We have been sanctified." Believers have been made holy; we have been set apart; we have been cleansed to the point of enabling us to enter into relationship with holy God! In case his audience missed the implication of his choice of verb tense, the author of Hebrews spells it out: "One sacrifice for sins *for all time.*" Two verses later he uses this same phrase again:

> For by one offering He has perfected *for all time* those who are sanctified. —*Hebrews 10:14, emphasis mine*

From this passage, two things are unmistakably clear. First, Christians were sanctified or made holy through the death of Christ—a process that never needs to be repeated. Second, those who were sanctified have been perfected, or had their guilt removed, *for all time.* That means forever! It is no wonder that the author follows up this discussion with these words:

Think About It

If Christ was the sacrifice for sin, and yet at the time of his death all your sins were yet to be committed, which of your sins did His blood cover?
From the vantage point of the Cross, was there really any difference between the sins you committed in the past and those you will commit in the future?

Let us draw near with a sincere *heart in full assurance* of faith,
having our hearts sprinkled clean from an evil conscience and
our bodies washed with pure water. Let us hold fast the confession of our hope without wavering, for He who promised is
faithful.   —*Hebrews 10:22-23, emphasis mine*

This passage is just one of many in the book of Hebrews
that demonstrates the author's confidence in the security
of the believer. Again, this view rests not on a few verses
but on the entire tone and flow of the book.

To say that Christians can lose salvation is to say that
the blood of Christ was *inadequate* to perfect for all time
those whom God has sanctified. To say that is to equate
His blood with the blood of bulls and goats. And that is an
equation I doubt many human beings would be comfortable making.

Our whole discussion boils down to this one question,
"Was the blood of Christ adequate?" During my own struggles with eternal security, this question used to haunt me.
I knew then as I do now that to accept His blood as the
adequate payment for my sin settled the question once
and for all. On the other hand, to say His blood was not
adequate sounded like blasphemy.

I can remember a discussion I had with a missionary
who did not believe in once saved always saved. When I
posed the question to him he said, "Yes, Charles, Christ's
blood was adequate, but we have to do our part as well."
For him, "our part" included a consistent walk with God—
which really boiled down to works.

He had attempted to do what so many tried in the past:
to introduce a third alternative. But there is no third
choice. Christ's blood was either adequate or it was not.
*To qualify the affirmative answer to this question is to af-
firm the negative.* If my salvation hinges on Christ's blood
and "my part," then it is plain to see that His blood was
not adequate. But I have never met anyone who claimed
to be a Christian who would admit that. It sounds too he-
retical.

Hebrews is clear. Christ's blood was adequate to perfect for all time those whom God has sanctified. We need add nothing to it. *Our part* is simply to respond to His unconditional love with reverence and obedience, while resting in the assurance that our eternity is secure.

Notes

1. Homer A. Kent, *The Epistle to the Hebrews* (Grand Rapids, Mich.: Baker, 1972), p. 185. Kent explains the author's use of the perfect tense and its meaning.

Do You Know?

1. *What does the phrase* to make perfect *mean?*
2. *Why were animal sacrifices unsatisfactory?*
3. *Does the Bible say that once a person experiences absolute cleansing, he or she is no longer aware of sin? What does the reference to "consciousness of sins" in Hebrews 10:2 mean?*
4. *What are some of the passages in Hebrews that demonstrate the security of believers?*

19

Warning 1:
No Escape

For this reason we must pay much closer attention to what we have heard, lest we drift away from it. For if the word spoken through angels proved unalterable, and every transgression and disobedience received a just recompense, how shall we escape if we neglect so great a salvation? After it was at the first spoken through the Lord, it was confirmed to us by those who heard.
— *Hebrews 2:1–3*

After a convincing presentation of Christ's superiority to the angels, the author of Hebrews seizes the opportunity to apply this truth to the lives of his readers. He begins with a stern word of exhortation followed by a warning. His readers must "pay much closer attention" to the things they have heard. Otherwise, they will be prone to "drift away."

What follows is a short, nondetailed description of the consequences of *drifting away.* This account of what happens once a person drifts has caused some to doubt the concept of eternal security. They understand the author to be threatening his readers with the loss of their salvation if they drift away from the truth.

Drifting

The author addresses his audience as a teacher would address a class of students. The term *drift* literally refers to something carried away by a current of water or air. But here the author uses it the way a teacher would use the term when referring to a student whose attention had drifted away from the subject matter or an athlete whose dedication to his sport was waning because his attention was drifting toward another pursuit.

The term *drifting* implies a slow, gradual process. The author realized that something was competing for his audience's attention. They had the potential of losing interest in the things pertaining to salvation through Christ. Like a teacher who notices a student staring out the window, the author firmly says, "Pay attention!"

The Comparison

Every teacher knows that to make a warning effective, there must be an "or else." A student must know the consequences of ignoring the demands of his or her superior if a warning is to be taken seriously. The author of Hebrews states his "or else" in the form of a comparison. He compares the consequences of ignoring "the word spoken through angels" to the consequences of ignoring the message of Christ Himself. To paraphrase, "If you think it was bad for those who ignored God's message when it was communicated through angels, imagine how it is going to be for men and women who ignore a message that comes directly from His Son!"

The "word" spoken through angels in all probability refers to the Old Testament law.[1] The author argues that if the law, which came by way of angels, had clearly delineated penalties for those who disobeyed, how much greater penalty must there be for disobeying the commands of the Son of God? He increases the weight of his warning by pointing to the extra measures God took to validate the truth of Christ's message:

God also bearing witness with them, both by signs and wonders and by various miracles and by gifts of the Holy Spirit according to His will.   —*Hebrews 2:4*

Or Else . . .

The author of Hebrews is somewhat vague at this point. He goes to great lengths to emphasize that there will be a penalty for neglecting the message of Christ, but he doesn't explain what the penalty might be. One of three things is true: He did not know what would happen, he knew but did not want to tell, or he assumed his readers already knew.

If his goal was to motivate a wandering body of believers—a group he knew personally and cared a great deal for—and he knew the penalty for drifting was the loss of salvation, surely he would have spelled it out; it was certainly not a good time to leave them guessing. And what could be more motivating than the potential loss of one's eternal salvation? Yet the author simply states, "How shall we escape," without telling us exactly what we will not escape!

Apples and Oranges

There is another reason this passage cannot be referring to the loss of one's salvation. The author is comparing the penalty of breaking the Mosaic law with the penalty of "drifting away" from the message of Christ. The law had nothing to do with one's eternal salvation. Breaking the law in no way jeopardized one's eternal security. The penalties for violating the Mosaic law were all temporal in nature. The law was given to God's people—a people of faith—as a standard by which to conduct their daily affairs. Along with "do's" and "don'ts" there was a detailed list of "or else's." As the writer of Hebrews states, "Every transgression and disobedience received a just recompense" (2:2).

A man who broke any part of the law knew exactly the punishment to expect; it was all there for anyone to read.

Think About It

*A man does not drift
into salvation.
Does it really make sense
that he can drift
out of it?*

The punishments ranged from paying a fine to losing one's life. It all depended on the severity of the crime. Nowhere, however, did the law bring into question a man's eternal destiny. A man did not gain heaven by keeping the law. He did not miss it by breaking it.

Those who would use this passage to support an argument against eternal security miss the author's point altogether. He is warning believers. Just as Old Testament believers were chastened when they "drifted away" or disobeyed the law, so New Testament believers would be chastened as well—only more vigorously! Why? Because the revelation we are responsible for came directly from the Son. There is not the first implication that a loss of salvation is in view here. There is no mention of heaven, hell, judgment, or any of the other things associated with the eternal destiny of a man.

No One Escapes!

The author addresses an extremely important principle in these four verses. Unfortunately the debate surrounding them causes many people to miss the writer's intended meaning. As a pastor, I have seen this principle at work over and over again. As a Christian, I have seen this principle at work in my life. When a believer begins to drift away from the teachings of Christ, it is only a matter of time until the loving and yet firm hand of God goes to work to get the person's attention. No one "escapes." For some, it may take years; for others, days.

From time to time individuals and sometimes families will drop out of worship attendance. Several months later I will see them back at their regular set. Sometimes I will call just to let them know how pleased I am to see them back in church and to find out if something happened to cause them to leave. It is amazing how often I hear something along the lines of, "Well, nothing really happened. I guess we just kind of drifted away for a while. But we're back now." In each case, God moved in to get their attention.

God uses various means to bring His children into line: sickness, accidents, sermons, songs, confrontation by a friend, the loss of a loved one. Sometimes it comes in the form of an unexpected tragedy. At other times it is simply the natural consequences of whatever sin they have fallen into. We would all do well to heed the writer's warning and "pay much closer attention" to what we have heard, for we all have the potential to drift. And none of us will escape the consequences.

Notes

1. Homer A. Kent, *The Epistle to the Hebrews* (Grand Rapids, Mich.: Baker, 1972), p. 48. Kent presents substantial evidence for this view, including information to support the notion that such a view was generally accepted among first-century Jews.

Do You Know?

1. *What reasons could there be for the writer of Hebrews not explaining the penalty for neglecting the message of Christ?*
2. *Why is it unlikely that the penalty was the loss of salvation?*
3. *How does the author interpret the phrase, "no one escapes"?*
4. *What are some of the means that God uses to bring His children into line?*

20

Warning 2: Falling Away

For in the case of those who have once been enlightened and have tasted of the heavenly gift and have been made partakers of the Holy Spirit, and have tasted the good word of God and the power of the age to come, and then have fallen away, it is impossible to renew them again to repentance, since they again crucify to themselves the Son of God, and put Him to open shame.
—Hebrews 6:4–6

As we mentioned earlier, this passage is probably used more than any other to support the idea that salvation can be lost. At a glance these verses do appear to support that view. But unfortunately for those who do not believe in eternal security, these verses seem to go a step beyond what they believe.

If the subject of these verses is salvation, believers who "fall away" can never be saved again! There is no second chance. In the author's words, "It is impossible to renew them again to repentance."

Traditional Arminian teaching has always provided an opportunity for a man or a woman to be born again and again—and for that matter again and again and again. Few believe that salvation can be lost and never regained.

True Believers

Some commentators assert that this passage refers to those who have been exposed to Christian truth but were never genuinely converted. If that were the case, this passage would pose little problem. It seems to me, however, the writer bends over backward to make sure the reader understands that the persons he is describing are genuine, born-again believers.

The individuals had been "enlightened." The author uses this same term again in the tenth chapter where it is clearly used to refer to believers (see Heb. 10:32). Consistency would argue for the reference in the sixth chapter to be to true believers as well.

The expression "have tasted of the heavenly gift" uses the term *tasted* in such a way as to denote "experienced." One commentator writes,

> The verb itself did not mean a mere sampling, but a real experience, as its use in Acts 10:10 attests. The writer of Hebrews has already used "tasted" in the sense of experienced in 2:9 where "Christ tasted death." Surely the meaning is that He actually experienced it.[1]

There is some question about what the "heavenly gift" actually is. Some say salvation, some say the Holy Spirit, and others argue that it is forgiveness. Regardless of what it refers to, the individuals had a real dose of it; they had experienced the heavenly gift.

Probably the strongest argument for these persons being genuine Christians is the author's next statement: "And have been made partakers of the Holy Spirit." Earlier in Hebrews the author talks about his audience being "partakers of a heavenly calling" and "partakers of Christ." In these instances there seems to be no doubt he is referring to authentic Christians. Once again, consistency would argue for his use of "partakers" in chapter 6 to be referring to persons who had experienced the indwelling presence of the Holy Spirit.

Once again, the author uses the term *tasted*. This time, however, the objects are more clearly defined: "And have tasted the good word of God and the powers of the age to come." The individuals under consideration had to some degree experienced the Word of God and had seen the power of God demonstrated in their lives. Aren't these primarily the experiences of believers?

If the persons "fall away," it is impossible to "renew them again to repentance." "Fall away" is understood to mean turn away from Christ. It is not clear whether the author has in mind a sudden abandonment of the faith or a gradual drifting away as he warns of earlier (see Heb. 2:1). Either way, the individuals lost all hope of ever entering heaven. They lost salvation.

The Author's Concern

As we work our way back through these verses, keep in mind that the people being addressed were primarily Jewish Christians. The author's fear was not that they would consciously turn their backs on God and fall into sin. His fear was that they would consciously turn away from Christ and without knowing it have turned their backs on God as well. There was a great deal more at stake than his readers realized. They were under the impression that they could just return to their old ways of life, including their original form of worship. They thought they would be returning to the God of their fathers. The author of Hebrews, however, knew that they were actually abandoning the God of their fathers.

In the remaining chapters of Hebrews you can feel the intensity with which the author writes. He wants desperately for his audience to come to grips with who Christ is, the ultimate High Priest, the once and for all sacrifice for sin.

The Warning

"Fallen away" clearly implies apostasy; the writer was describing the plight of people who had gone so far as to abandon the faith entirely. Whereas the majority of his

Think About It

If Hebrews 6:6 is talking about renewing a person's salvation, doesn't this passage teach that once a person loses salvation, he or she can never regain it?

If that is the case, aren't we doing children a great disservice by encouraging them to be born again? Shouldn't we wait until they are much older to lessen the likelihood that they fall away during their teen years and thus lose their salvation forever?

audience were not to that point yet (see Heb. 6:9), the author felt the need to inform them of where they were headed.

The persons described in these verses were genuine, born-again believers. As followers of Christ, they had experienced the Christian life in its fullest sense. They had seen the power of God at work in their lives and in the lives of others. Then for some unexplained reason they began doubting the claims of Christ. That continued until finally they turned their backs on all that they at one time embraced and returned to Judaism.

Repentance

According to the author of Hebrews, it is impossible for persons in this state to be "brought back" (NIV) to repentance. The author points to the absolute impossibility of any outside force changing their minds: they are beyond convincing.

It is equally important to notice what the author does not say. He does not say that the individuals cannot be *forgiven* or restored to *salvation*.[2] The issue here is *repentance*. Repentance has to do with changing one's mind. Dr. Ryrie, in his excellent book *So Great Salvation,* has this to say about repentance:

> In both the Old and New Testaments *repentance* means "to change one's mind." But the question must be asked, About what do you change your mind? Answering that question will focus the meaning on the particular change involved. . . . *First* there can be repentance that either has no relation to eternal salvation or at least does not result in salvation. . . . *Second,* there is repentance that is unto salvation. . . . A *third* category of uses of the word *repent* concerns repentance within the experience of Christian living.[3]

It is a mistake to assume that the author has salvation in mind here simply because he uses the term *repentance*.

The context argues for a different understanding altogether. Simply put, those who used to think one way about Christ but now think another way about Him are beyond convincing; their minds cannot be changed.

To illustrate this point even further, think for a moment about the most committed Christian you know. Now imagine that this individual abandoned the faith and you were given the responsibility of convincing her to return to Christ. What would you say? She knows all the verses. She has seen and even experienced what God can do in a life. She has already heard the war stories about what happens to people who live their lives apart from Christ. No doubt she has done enough counseling to guess where your questions are leading. What would you do? What could you say that would really make any difference?

Several years ago a friend of mine in another city called to ask me to help his church. Their pastor had become romantically involved with a woman in his church. When the liaison became public, he resigned his position at the church and announced that he was divorcing his wife and marrying his girlfriend. "Dr. Stanley," he said, "I think he may listen to you. Would you drive up here and visit him?" I knew I had to go.

I walked into his office unannounced and sat down. He was quite surprised to see me. Neither of us said anything for several minutes. He knew why I was there. I really had no choice. But it became apparent to me there was nothing I could say that he did not already know. He knew what Jesus said about divorce. He knew about the judgment seat of Christ. He had heard plenty of testimonies of how God's grace can heal a marriage. He had talked to pastors who had gotten out of the ministry only to regret it later. He knew the effects of his actions on his kids. He had read all the right books, heard all the right tapes, and exegeted all the pertinent verses. Yet his mind was made up. I stayed about ten minutes. I do not regret going. But it did no good. He left his wife and married the other woman. Nothing or no one could have made him *change his mind* about his marriage or his ministry. His mind was made up. He was beyond convincing.

So it was with the Jews to whom the writer of Hebrews is referring. There was nothing to say to them. Their minds were made up. They had seen both sides and decided to retreat back to Judaism, unaware that they were turning their backs on the very God to whom they intended to return.

The Reason Why

In the second half of verse 6 the writer tells us why these people cannot be brought to repentance:

> Since they again crucify to themselves the Son of God, and put Him to open shame.

"Since" carries a causal force. The New International Version uses "because," which more accurately communicates the author's idea.

By turning their backs on Christ, these Jews were in essence agreeing with the Jews who had Christ arrested and ultimately put to death. If He was not THE Christ—and apparently they did not think He was—He was a false Christ and deserved to die. The phrase "to themselves" is the author's way of pointing out the group's attitude. Insofar as they were concerned, Jesus deserved to die.

Since they had at one point publicly professed Christ as their Savior and thus the Messiah, their public denial would bring shame on those who maintained their belief in Christ. Outsiders would conclude that there must not be much to Christianity if those who at one time said they believed changed their minds and went back to their former religion.

The Most Amazing Grace

If one takes seriously the original context of the writer's statements, it is clear that this solemn warning in no way threatens the security of the believer. Actually, it is evidence *for* the believer's security. If a Jew, who was awaiting the coming of the Messiah, could find salvation through Christ and then walk away from Him without the threat of losing his or her salvation, what do the rest of us have to fear? No other group had more revelation concerning the coming of the Messiah. Their whole culture was centered on God's law and His promises about ultimate salvation from sin. For a Jew to come face to face with the claims of Christ and to accept them for a while and then walk away seems unforgivable. But our ways are not His ways—and it's a good thing they aren't!

The writer of Hebrews offers a serious warning. It is a dangerous thing for a believer to turn his back on Christ. To do so is to run the risk of drifting beyond the point of return—not a return to salvation, but a return to fellowship with the Savior.

Notes

1. Homer A. Kent, *The Epistle to the Hebrews* (Grand Rapids, Mich.: Baker, 1972), p. 108.
2. *The Expositors Bible Commentary, Hebrews,* vol. 12 (Grand Rapids, Mich.: Zondervan, 1981), p. 55.
3. Charles C. Ryrie, *So Great Salvation* (Wheaton, Ill.: Victor Books, 1989), pp. 92–99. In these pages Dr. Ryrie gives scriptural examples of all three uses of the term *repentance.*

Do You Know?

1. *What does the writer of Hebrews mean when he uses the term* fallen away? *What does the term imply?*
2. *What are the three categories of the use of the word* repentance *discussed by Charles Ryrie?*
3. *Is the security of believers threatened by their falling away?*
4. *Why is it dangerous for believers to turn their backs on Christ?*

21

Warning 3: No More Offering

For if we go on sinning willfully after receiving the knowledge of the truth, there no longer remains a sacrifice for sins, but a certain terrifying expectation of judgment, and the *fury of a fire which will consume the adversaries.* Anyone who has set aside the Law of Moses dies without mercy on the testimony of two or three witnesses. How much severer punishment do you think he will deserve who has trampled under foot the Son of God, and has regarded as unclean the blood of the covenant by which he was sanctified, and has insulted the Spirit of grace? For we know Him who said, "Vengeance is Mine, I will repay." And again, "The Lord will judge His people." It is a terrifying thing to fall into the hands of the living God.
                                                    —*Hebrews 10:26–31, emphasis mine*

Isolated from its context, this stern warning can be easily interpreted to teach the possibility of losing one's salvation. After all, it says quite plainly that there is no provision for the sin of those who go on sinning after receiving the knowledge of the truth. Furthermore, they can expect a fiery judgment. Again, in isolation, this passage certainly seems to pose a problem to our thesis.

Going, Going, Gone

For the sake of argument, let's assume for the moment that this is the proper interpretation of this passage. Several questions immediately surface. For instance, if we take the passage at face value—without qualifying it as many do—any intentional or willful sin we commit after

171

we have received the truth eliminates our potential for being forgiven. After all, if forgiveness comes through a sacrifice for sin, and there is no more sacrifice for sin, there is no forgiveness.

One may argue, "This passage applies only to those whose life-style is characterized by sin." In other words, there remains a sacrifice for sin if there are only a few sins or if they are spread out over time. The problems here are twofold. First, nothing in the Greek text justifies a translation implying that the author has a *life-style* in mind here. The King James Version is the most accurate when it says, "If we sin willfully."[1] Again, anyone who sins willfully cannot expect another sacrifice for sins.

Second, the Bible never makes a distinction between which sins Christ's death paid for. If there is a sacrifice for a few sins, why not a sacrifice for all the sins a Christian commits? The author's point is clear: There is no more sacrifice for sins of any kind for anybody. He writes,

> But He, having offered one sacrifice for sins for all time, sat down at the right hand of God, waiting from that time onward until His enemies be made a footstool for His feet. For by one offering He has perfected for all time those who are sanctified.
> —*Hebrews 10:12–14*

Jesus is out of the sacrificing business. He is waiting, seated beside His Father. The next time He stands up, He will assume the role of a Judge, not a Lamb. If this passage teaches that willful sin results in the loss of salvation, it also teaches that salvation is lost over one willful sin. Furthermore, once it is lost, it is lost forever because there is no more sacrifice for sin.

Those who use such passages to validate their disbelief in eternal security rarely take their interpretations to their logical ends. I have never met anyone who believed a Christian could lose salvation *once and for all* over any single willful sin.

View Number Two

The passage begins with the word *for,* which relates it to what immediately preceded it. In the verses leading up to the warning, the author encourages his audience to follow through with their commitment to Christ in light of all He has done for them. He makes two particularly important statements in this section:

> Let us draw near with a sincere heart . . . having our hearts sprinkled clean from an evil conscience and our bodies washed with pure water. —*Hebrews 10:22*

And then he declares,

> Let us hold fast the confession of our hope without wavering, for He who promised is faithful. —*Hebrews 10:23*

Following these verses, he applies the principles within them:

> And let us consider how to stimulate one another to love and good deeds, not forsaking our own assembling together, as is the habit of some, but encouraging one another; and all the more, as you see the day drawing near. —*Hebrews 10:24-25*

The "day" he mentions is the second coming of Christ.

The logical questions after these words of exhortation and encouragement would be, But what if we do waver? What if we don't follow through? What will happen if we drop out of the fellowship? Anticipating their questions, he describes exactly what they could and could not expect.

Great Expectations

Remember, the people in the audience are primarily Jewish. All their lives they had waited for a Messiah. One

Think About It

*If there is no longer
any sacrifice for sins,
and the sacrifice for sins
took place at Calvary,
for which of your sins
was sacrifice made?*

who would come and take away their sins. One who would establish a new covenant, a covenant so powerful that as a result God would forget their sins forever (see Heb. 10:17).

Whereas we today look back to the Cross for forgiveness, these men and women were in the habit of looking ahead for forgiveness. When we sin, we are grateful Christ has forgiven us. When they sinned, they were hopeful that the Messiah would one day come and forgive them. As you can imagine, this would have been a difficult habit for them to break. The fact that they had never seen Christ or heard Him teach would have made it especially difficult.

In keeping with his theme of Christ as Messiah, the author of Hebrews takes this opportunity to remind his audience yet another time that the sacrifice they had been awaiting had already taken place. To paraphrase, "If you willfully sin, remember that the next scheduled event is an encounter not with Christ the Savior but with Christ the Judge."

The statement, "There no longer remains a sacrifice for sins," is not meant to be negative. The writer says the same thing in verse 18. There the mood of the text is clearly positive. It is good news. The bad news is that God is not fond of quitters.

Fire

Verse 27 immediately brings to mind 1 Corinthians 3. Once again a biblical writer uses the coming judgment as motivation for godly living. The imagery of fire is neither new nor inappropriate here, for the Christian will be tried by fire. Notice, too, that the fire here is connected not with punishment but with judgment.[2]

At this point the author takes advantage of his audience's extensive knowledge of the law to illustrate the severity of this judgment. In essence he says, "If you think it was bad for those who despised the law, imagine how bad

175

it will be for those who despised the Son of the Law Giver!"

In verse 29 the author exposes the willful sin of the believer for everything it is. No doubt his readers were shocked as they read this description. Like us, they had overlooked the implications of their sin. They had not realized the insult to the grace of God and the blood of Christ that every sin carried with it. Now they understood the severity of the coming judgment. They were beginning to understand the implications of being post-Cross believers. It was one thing to sin knowing that one day the Messiah would come and do away with sin's penalty. It was another thing altogether to sin after the penalty was paid.

Many penalties are worse than death. This truth is especially easy to comprehend when we think in terms of eternity. Everyone is going to die; even righteous men die. To stand at the judgment seat of Christ and see our works burned to ashes would be a "much severer punishment" than death (Heb. 10:29). For believers who live for themselves with little or no thought for the things of God, it will certainly be a "terrifying thing to fall into the hands of the living God."

A Look to the Future

Whoever labeled this a warning passage was correct in doing so. It is not, however, a warning to believers that their salvation is in jeopardy. The context and the details of the text rule that out as a valid interpretation.

The author of Hebrews is warning his Jewish audience of the consequences of willful disobedience to Christ. They can no longer justify their sin in light of the coming Messiah. He has already come. In their next encounter with the Messiah, He will stand as a Judge who will hand down decisions based on the new covenant.

This passage stands as a stern warning to non-Jewish believers today as well. We are reminded that every moment and every decision count. Nothing goes unnoticed. And for those who think that they are getting by with something, recall these words: "It is a terrifying thing to fall into the hands of the living God."

Notes

1. *The Bible Knowledge Commentary,* "NT," Walvoord and Zurk (Wheaton, Ill.: Victor Books, 1983), p. 805.
2. In passages dealing with the judgment of non-Christians, fire is often associated with their punishment but not their judgment (see Rev. 20:11–15; 21:7–8). It seems incorrect to say that non-Christians are judged by fire.

Do You Know?

1. What does the writer of Hebrews mean by the statement, "there no longer remains a sacrifice for sins"?
2. Is it possible to lose salvation once and for all over any single willful sin?
3. What penalty would be a "much severer punishment" than death?
4. How does continued sin insult the grace of God and blood of Christ?

22

Does God Have an Eraser?

He who overcomes shall thus be clothed in white garments;
and I will not erase his name from the book of life.
—*Revelation 3:5*

This passage is often cited to cast doubt on the doctrine
of eternal security. The argument runs something like this:
- The Bible teaches that those who overcome will not
  have their names erased from the book of life.
- Not every believer is an overcomer.
- Therefore, those who do not overcome run the risk of
  having their names erased from the book of life.
- If it is impossible for anyone's name to be erased,
  what is the point of saying a particular group will not
  be erased?
- Besides, David prayed that the names of his enemies
  would be blotted out of the book of life (see Ps.
  69:28).

On the surface this argument appears to be a strong one
in favor of those who believe salvation can be lost. We will
begin our investigation of this line of reasoning by looking
first at what the New Testament has to say concerning the
book of life. Then we will examine David's prayer in Psalm
69.

Congratulations!

It is unfortunate that this passage in Revelation has become a focal point of controversy. The result has been a

fixation on what the verse does *not* say rather than what it does say. This verse was never intended as a warning. Within its context there is nothing negative or foreboding about these words. In fact, it makes a strong statement in favor of eternal security. It is a passage of encouragement and praise.

The comments are directed to a group of faithful believers from the church in Sardis. Unlike the majority of the folks in their congregation, this handful of members had remained unsoiled by the world around them. The verse in question contains Christ's commendation to this group for their consistent walk.

To assume from what is said here that God will possibly erase names from the book of life is to read into the text a concept clearly not present. At best, it is an argument from silence, for the verse simply reads, "And I will not erase his name from the book of life."[1] If this statement raises doubts for some about eternal security, they would do well to search the Scriptures for an answer. But to *base* one's answer to this important question on this verse is to adopt a method of study with the potential of leading to all kinds of problematic conclusions.

First Printing

The apostle John refers to the "book of life" five other times in Revelation.[2] From two of these passages it becomes evident that he certainly did not believe names could be erased:

> And all who dwell on the earth will worship him, everyone whose name has not been *written from the foundation of the world* in the book of life of the Lamb who has been slain.
> —*Revelation 13:8, emphasis mine*

> And those who dwell on the earth will wonder, whose name has not been written in the book of life from the *foundation of the world.*
> —*Revelation 17:8, emphasis mine*

In these passages John informs us about the time when the book of life was filled out. This information comes as a surprise. Without it, our assumption would be that when men or women put their trust in Christ, their names were added at that moment. But that is not the case at all. The book of life has been complete since the foundation of the world.

By "world," John does not mean "earth." In both passages "earth" and "world" appear. These are from two different Greek words. The one translated "earth" means just that—this ball of dirt upon which we live. The Greek word translated "world" is *kosmos* from which we get our English word *cosmos.*

John is using "world" here to refer to the entire universe (see John 1:3; Acts 17:24). In light of the scientific limitations of John's day, it could very well be a reference to all created things. Either way, his point is the same: *The book of life was filled out before the first entry was ever born.*

If that is the case, God's foreknowledge had a great deal to do with who was written in and who was not. In anticipation of Christ's death on man's behalf, God wrote the names of those He knew from eternity past would accept His gracious offer. The apostle Paul had this same idea in mind when he wrote,

> Just as He chose us in Him before the foundation of the world, that we should be holy and blameless before Him.
> —*Ephesians 1:4*

God wrote before we *did* anything. He filled out the book of life in anticipation of what He knew we would do. Therefore, He did not write in response to what we *actually* did; rather, He wrote in response to what He *knew* we would actually do.

This distinction is very important. For if God put names in the book as history unfolded—as we actually believed

Think About It

*Does it make any sense
to say that salvation
is offered as a solution
for our sin and then
to turn around and teach
that salvation can be
taken away
because of our sin
as well?*

—it could be argued that He erases them as history unfolds as well. But if God entered names according to His foreknowledge, it follows that He would erase them according to His foreknowledge, which makes no sense at all. If God wrote and erased according to foreknowledge, both His writing and His erasing would be complete before the world began. In that case, no one needs to live with the fear that his or her name will be erased from the book of life sometime in the future. But if that is the case, Revelation 3:5 is no longer a problem.

Missing Persons

There is a second reason these passages eliminate the possibility of names being erased. Both passages indicate that the lost people in these verses had never had their names written in the book of life. John does not say these names were simply not in the book at that time. He says, "Everyone whose name has not been written from the foundation of the world."

Who is he talking about here? "All who dwell on the earth." In other words, no lost persons alive at that time had *ever* had their names in the book of life. Of course, they had never had their names erased from the book, either.

The only way around this problem for those who hold to the *erasable name view* is to maintain that all the unsaved people who had their names erased were already dead by this time in history. That is certainly possible, but it is highly unlikely. It is especially unlikely in light of the intense persecution those who name the name of Christ will be facing during this time (see Rev. 13:7).

Good News

The good news is, God's pencil has no eraser. Before you breathed your first word, God knew how you would respond to His offer of grace. According to His foreknowledge, He wrote your name in the book of life. And there it shall remain forever. Jesus said it this way:

> My sheep hear My voice, and I know them, and they follow me; and I give eternal life to them, and they shall never perish; and no one shall snatch them out of My hand. —*John 10:27–28*

And as if that were not clear enough:

> My Father, who has given them to Me, is greater than all; and no one is able to snatch them out of the Father's hand.
> —*John 10:29*

It would seem that such clear statements would make books like this one unnecessary. Maybe one day that will be the case.

Notes

1. Some have argued that John is employing a figure of speech known as *litotes*. A litotes is an understatement in which an affirmative is expressed by the negative of the contrary. A modern example would be a baseball coach's saying to a player who just hit a grand slam, "Well, son, I guess you're not a bad player." The coach is simply complimenting his star player. To paraphrase what John is trying to get across in 3:5, "You who have remained faithful will certainly not have your names erased; on the contrary, you will be announced by name to the Father."
   Zane Hodges cites Hebrews 6:10 and Revelation 2:11 as other examples of litotes. See *Grace in Eclipse*, pp. 109–10.
2. Concerning the textual options in Revelation 22:19, I am in agreement with the editors of the NASB and NIV who chose the reading "tree of life" rather than "the book of life." Other verses in Revelation that refer to "the book of life" are 3:5; 20:12, 15; 21:27.

Do You Know?

1. *What is a* litotes? *Give some examples from Scripture and from everyday life.*
2. *When did God write the names in the book of life?*
3. *What does the author mean when he talks about God's* foreknowledge?
4. *Why does it make "no sense" to fear that God will erase your name from the book of life?*

23

Recorded with the Righteous

Do Thou add iniquity to their iniquity,
And may they not come into Thy righteousness,
May they be blotted out of the book of life,
And may they not be recorded with the righteous.
                                                —*Psalm 69:27–28*

David's enemies had finally pushed him over the limit. He had grown weary of dealing with them. He was fed up with their gossip and slanderous lies. He was ready for God to take serious action against them. So he asked that they be blotted out of the book of life.

These verses, like Revelation 3:5, have caused some to feel insecure about the permanency of their salvation. That's understandable. For here we find King David asking God to blot his enemies' names out of the book of life. Surely he would not request such a thing if he did not believe it was possible.

In light of what we discovered in our study of Revelation 3:5, it would be tempting to handle this passage by saying David was simply mistaken in his request; maybe he didn't know God was not in the habit of blotting people's names out of His book.

This appraisal, however, raises questions concerning the inspiration of the psalm. If David was being guided by the Holy Spirit as he wrote, it is doubtful he would be led to ask something outside the realm of theological possibility (see 2 Pet. 1:21). David knew what he was praying all right. And as we will see, his request was clearly within the framework of God's normal activity.

Making Old Things New

This passage and others like it pose such a problem for us because we have a tendency to interpret them from a New Testament perspective. That is, we take what we know from the New Testament and read it back into these Old Testament verses. Instead of seeking to discover what Old Testament authors meant by certain words and phrases, we jump right in and interpret them in keeping with New Testament usage.

In this case we have taken the phrase "book of life" as it appears in Psalm 69 and interpreted it according to what the New Testament says about the "book of life." We have assumed that the book of life David is referring to is the same as that mentioned in Revelation. A more accurate approach would be to ask, What did David have in mind by the phrase "book of life"? To answer that question, we would turn not to the New Testament but to other portions of the Old Testament.

Books, Books, and More Books

The ancient Hebrews viewed God as a great Record Keeper. They pictured Him having in His possession a book with a list of all living people. Whether they believed it was a literal book or not is beside the point. They referred to this book in their literature in the same way the New Testament authors refer to the book of life.

Anyone who has read much of the Old Testament knows that names and geneaologies were very important to the Jews, who took this type of record keeping very seriously. That is why such references are scattered throughout the Old Testament as well as in the beginning of Matthew and Luke. The Jews assumed God kept good records as well, which He does. The Old Testament writers make frequent reference to this divine practice. Five passages of particular interest come right out of the book of Psalms:

> The LORD shall count when He registers the peoples,
> "This one was born there."
>   *—Psalm 87:6*

> Thou hast taken account of my wanderings;
> Put my tears in Thy bottle;
> Are they not in *Thy book?* *—Psalm 56:8, emphasis mine*

> My frame was not hidden from Thee,
> When I was made in secret,
> And skillfully wrought in the depths of the earth.
> Thine eyes have seen my unformed substance;
> And in *Thy book* they were all written,
> The days that were ordained for me,
> When as yet there was not one of them.
>   *—Psalm 139:15–16, emphasis mine*

> According to the greatness of Thy compassion blot out my transgressions.   *—Psalm 51:1*

Some interesting things surface from these verses. In the first passage we learn that God has a register in which He keeps a head count of the living. In the second passage we read that God records the events of our lives. In the third passage we discover that God has a record book containing the number of days ordained for each person's life.

In Psalm 51 the term *book* is not actually used. However, the phrase "blot out" is. These are the same words used in Psalm 69 where David talks about blotting out the names of his enemies. To blot something out is to erase it. Psalm 51 implies that God has a record book for sin as well.

With all these references to books in Psalms, not once

Think About It

*Can joy and insecurity
really coexist? How realistic
is it to expect
us to rejoice over
a relationship that is only
as secure as our behavior
is consistent?*

do we run across a book described as containing the names of the saved as opposed to the unsaved.[1] The closest thing to it is found in the passage under consideration when David writes, "And may they not be recorded with the righteous."

When David refers to the "book of life" in Psalm 69, he is talking about God's record of the living. "Life" is a reference to physical life, not eternal life. This interpretation is consistent with the verses we looked at from Psalm 139. David is not asking God to send his enemies to hell. He simply wants their lives shortened.

Several elements from the text support this interpretation. First of all, the other things David asks God to do to his enemies are physical in nature (see vv. 22–26). He begins by appealing to God to send illness on them. Then he requests that their families suffer. Next he asks that their names be removed from the book of life. It's as if he builds up to the point of calling on God to go ahead and take them off the scene completely.

Second, to interpret "book of life" as the Lamb's book of life implies that David's enemies were believers. How else would they have gotten their names in the Lamb's book of life? But the entire psalm presents the people as unrighteous and wicked.

Third, in the previous verse, David asks that his enemies "not come into" God's righteousness (see Ps. 69:27). If their names were in the Lamb's book of life, they would have already come into His righteousness. Therefore, it would make better sense to understand this book as a list of the living, not a list of the righteous.

"Blot Me Out . . ."

Interestingly enough, David is not the only Old Testament figure who asked God to blot someone out of a book. Moses made a request to be blotted out:

> Then Moses returned to the LORD, and said, "Alas, this people has committed a great sin, and they have made a god of gold for themselves. But now, if Thou wilt, forgive their sin—and if not, please blot me out from Thy *book* which Thou hast written!" And the LORD said to Moses, "Whoever has sinned against Me, I will blot him out of My *book.*"—*Exodus 32:31–33, emphasis mine*

Here again, the "book" refers to a register of the living. Moses was asking God to take his physical life, not send him to hell. God, however, refused. But He promised to take the lives of those in the group who sinned against Him, and He did (see Exod. 32:35; Deut. 1:35–36; 2:14). Nowhere is it even hinted that those men and women were sent to hell.

On Again, Off Again

It would be rather disconcerting to think that a man after God's own heart would pray for the removal of someone's name from the Lamb's book of life. If you think about it, that really doesn't make much sense. For this same God sent His son into the world to save the world. And He paid a high price to make that salvation possible.

Our heavenly Father is in the business of getting names on the list, not taking them off. For those of us who are on the list, that is cause for great rejoicing. Jesus reminded His disciples of this when He said,

> Behold, I have given you authority to tread upon serpents and scorpions, and over all the power of the enemy, and nothing shall injure you. Nevertheless do not rejoice in this, that the spirits are subject to you, but rejoice that your names are recorded in heaven. —*Luke 10:19–20*

May this glorious truth become a source of assurance as well as joy.

Notes

1. Keil-Delitzsch, *Commentary on the Old Testament,* vol. 5 (Grand Rapids, Mich.: Eerdmans, reprinted 1982), p. 285. "For it is only in the New Testament that we meet with the book of life as a list of the names of the heirs of eternal life."

Do You Know?

1. *Is the* book of life *discussed in the Old Testament the same* book of life *discussed in the New Testament?*
2. *When David prayed that God would blot his enemies' names from the book of life, was he asking that his enemies be sent to hell? Explain.*
3. *Why did Moses ask God to blot him from His book? How did God respond?*
4. *How would you feel if someone after God's own heart —like Moses—could pray you out of heaven?*

Conclusion

I have never met a Christian who had lost his salvation. However, I have met plenty who had lost their assurance. Our *security* rests in the hands of an unconditionally loving heavenly Father. One who gave His best to insure our fellowship with Him forever. Our *assurance* rests in understanding and acceptance of these glorious truths.

For some people, the problem is erroneous teaching; for others, the problem is guilt. But whatever the reason, the result is the same—a lack of assurance. And when assurance goes, the basic building blocks of the relationship go also.

More is at stake than assurance. The very gospel itself comes under attack when the eternal security of the believer is questioned. Placing the responsibility for maintaining salvation on the believer is adding works to grace. Salvation would no longer be a gift. It would become a trade—our faithfulness for His faithfulness.

This is a far cry from the good news Jesus preached and Paul heralded. Their gospel was salvation by faith—and only by faith.

The salvation spoken of by Jesus and Paul takes place at one moment in time yet seals the believer for all time. This faith moves the Judge not only to forgive and pardon the sinner, but to adopt him into His own family as well.

As we contemplate all that has been offered to us through Christ, we are forced to wonder why. Why the mercy? Why the kindness? The only answer is love—love of such magnitude that all human illustrations fall short, love that is unconditional at its core with no hidden agendas and no fine print. God's love is such that He accepts us just the way we are but refuses to leave us there.

The more one meditates and reflects on the nature of this unconditional love, the more absurd it sounds when someone begins talking about losing it. Why would God take away something He offers unconditionally? It makes no sense at all.

Our expression of faith places us into an unconditional relationship with our heavenly Father. He makes this offer to all people everywhere. Some will choose to accept it by faith, others will reject it. But the offer remains. Such is the nature of His love.

Sure, there are those who will abuse such an offer. But so pure is His love that even then He will not go back on His word. He remains faithful to the faithless. Nothing can separate us from His love. No one can snatch us from His hand. Where sin abounds, grace *super*abounds. Anything less would be less than unconditional.

Yet even with all this God has not abandoned the concept of justice. For within His plan of salvation there are special rewards for those who respond to Him in like kind. Great is their reward in heaven. Eternity will not be the same for every believer. We will all stand and give an account of our lives. We will be judged according to our deeds, whether good or bad. Our rank in His future kingdom is being decided each and every day of our lives.

For those who have as their ambition to be pleasing to the Lord, this comes as great news. For those who are seeking to have their cake and eat it too, this is rather disheartening. And so it should be. God is not One to be mocked. There are no loopholes in His economy. Even within the context of His grace, we will still reap what we sow. But that sword cuts both ways. For those who sow seeds of faithfulness and obedience, their crop will yield enduring fruit. For those who sow seeds of disobedience and selfishness, their crop will fail to endure the fiery judgment. They will have nothing to show for their lives. They will be poor in the kingdom of heaven.

God has gone to great lengths to make our relationship with Him possible. Doing so cost Him His Son. But the sacrifice of His Son did far more than merely provide us with the possibility of such a relationship; it guaranteed the permanency of that relationship as well.

Your salvation is secure. My prayer is that you would experience the assurance of this precious and costly gift.

About the Author

Twice elected president of the Southern Baptist Convention, Charles Stanley is senior pastor of the 12,000-member First Baptist Church, Atlanta, and is a popular broadcast teacher on *In Touch*, a national TV and radio program. Stanley received his bachelor of arts degree from the University of Richmond, bachelor of divinity degree from Southwestern Theological Seminary, and master's and doctor's degrees of theology from Luther Rice Seminary. Stanley is the author of *How to Handle Adversity*, *Temptation*, *Forgiveness*, *How to Keep Your Kids on Your Team*, and *How to Listen to God*.